Buttermilk
and
Boxer Shorts

Michael,
   The years trip along do they not? Somehow I ended up being old and my memories of old times are keener than yesterday's.
   Neal Beard

Buttermilk and Boxer Shorts

Neal Beard

Copyright © 2011 by Neal Beard.

ISBN: Softcover   978-1-4628-5320-5
       Ebook   978-1-4628-5321-2

All rights reserved. No part of this book may be reproduced or transmitted in any form or by any means, electronic or mechanical, including photocopying, recording, or by any information storage and retrieval system, without permission in writing from the copyright owner.

This book was printed in the United States of America.

To order additional copies of this book, contact:
Xlibris Corporation
1-888-795-4274
www.Xlibris.com
Orders@Xlibris.com
97103

CONTENTS

1	Daddy Cussed'	7
2	First Grade at Bill Arp School—1946	10
3	Blazing Outhouse	12
4	Monk Eye's Mangy Mutt	14
5	Dead Man Eats a Potato	17
6	Hadacol, the Cure All	20
7	The Goat Whisperer	23
8	Monk Eye and the Cool Cat Caper	26
9	Juicy Fruit and the Women's Missionary Union	29
10	The Fly Convention	32
11	Family Funeral Fueding	35
12	Bologna, Britches and a Brindled Bull Dog	38
13	Buttermilk and Boxer Shorts	41
14	Jip and the Settin' Hen	43
15	Buster, Bees, and Bruton	45
16	The Red Rooster the Rolling Store and the Red Man	48
17	Painted Pig's Feet	51
18	Monk Eye and the Driverless Truck	54
19	The Christmas Pony	57
20	The Chitlin' Challenge	60
21	A Well, a Bell, and Uncle Dell	63
22	Tearing Down the Old Outhouse	65
23	Monk Eye's Monster Machine Mishap	67
24	Jake the Snake Ain't Jake	70
25	Papa's Plump Pungent Possum	73
26	The Bull Dog and the Dumb Bull	76
27	Monk Eye's Mohawk	79

28	The Ghost of Wild Bill	82
29	Crazy Crip and Cold Cider	85
30	The Flying 'Possum	88
31	The Sure Fire Red Hot Cure	90
32	The Genuine Official Red Ryder BB Gun	93
33	The Unstole Truck	96
34	The Supreme Court of Bill Arp	99
35	Monk Eye and the Fortune Teller	102
36	What Happened to the Running Board?	105
37	The Twice Stole Shotgun Shells	108
38	Monk Eye and the Star of Bethlehem	110
39	Monk Eye's Marble Meal	113
40	The Party Line	116
41	The Blue Tailed Yellow Jacket	119
42	Monk Eye's Giant Rabbit Box	122
43	Lesson Learned in a Watermelon Patch	125
44	Monk Eye, Mumblety Peg, and Mud	127
45	Saving Monkeye	130
46	That was No Lady, that was My Horse	133
47	A Day that will Live in Infamy	136
48	A Bulldog Named Colley	139
49	Big Bertha the Bitter Barber	142
50	From Tragedy to Triumph	145

1

DADDY CUSSED'

Daddy never swore. It was a rule with him. It was a discipline. It was a way of life. He said, "swearing reveals a lack of constraint and character."

He made an extraordinary exception on Saturday, October 20, 1945. We were moving from Atlanta to Bill Arp. Moving day has squeezed a squeal out of many a stalwart soul and it was Daddy's turn to have his mettle tested.

Mr. Kenny Smith moved us in his nineteen thirty eight Chevrolet ton and a half stake body truck. The first blow out occurred about ten miles into the trip—war rationing made it impossible to get good tires. Daddy helped change the tire. The second befell them less than a mile from our new home. They had to remove the wheel and take it to a service station in Douglasville. It was past noon when the truck, sporting a "new" worn out tire, got to our house.

Daddy's fragile nerves were further frayed by afternoon circumstances. Mama had packed sandwiches for our lunch. The lunch basket was in the back seat of daddy's nineteen thirty nine Chevrolet. A gluttonous Red Bone hound jumped through an open window and proceeded to scarf down our food.

Then, in setting up our new wood burning cook stove, Daddy pulled the protector from the chimney flue and soot like fine black snow dusted his sweaty body.

He smashed a finger assembling a bed, screeched like a goosed eagle and broke into "Sunday cussin". He didn't use proper profanity but he courted its close kin.

Mr. Renzo Duren, our new neighbor, had said to Daddy, "In Douglas county when you're cuttin' wood and accidentally hit the ground you'll strike gold—if you don't hit a rock." My five year old mind didn't grasp his jest about the rocky soil. I spent the afternoon searching for gold with Daddy's new ax. I didn't find any but I located a bounty of rocks.

By dark the move was complete. Daddy was finished too. He was ready to fire up the new stove so Mama could cook supper. He took the gold digging ax and went to the wood pile to split some stove wood.

That dull ax plunged him over the precipice of piety. He had dealt with two flat tires, a pilfered lunch, a soot shower, a throbbing thumb, hunger and weariness. Now his new ax was blunted beyond use. The ax got good distance catapulting across the garden.

Daddy passed up "Sunday cussin" and went for the real thing. I've never heard such a storm of swearing. It was virginal. It was original. It was poetic. It was flowery. It was loose jointed and hyphenated. It was professional. It had a demonic cadence. It was reminiscent of recent events at Hiroshima and Nagasaki. One wouldn't believe it was its maiden voyage. He went through his repertoire at least twice before he sputtered to a crash landing.

The next morning, embarrassed over losing control, he poured out an apology to us. Mama answered for us, "We ain't never heard you cuss before yesterday. I reckon if the only time you do is on moving day we can forget it." Time's plow has furrowed my brow but I haven't forgotten.

Daddy liked one day living forty years after the move. To my knowledge he never swore again—nor did he ever moved again.

2

FIRST GRADE AT BILL ARP SCHOOL—1946

I survived the bloodiest and best seven years of my life at the Bill Arp grammar school. My exposure to the rigor and vigor of education began there in 1946.

The old brick building had three class rooms, an auditorium, kitchen, lunchroom and porch. Toilet facilities were out back—a multi-hole outhouse for boys and one for girls. Playground equipment was the coal pile, a bent over flag pole and two basketball backboards with no hoops.

Miss Floy Stovall taught first and second grades in room one. Another teacher taught third, fourth and fifth grades in room two. The principal taught sixth and seventh grades in room three.

When weather prevented outside recess we played non-musical chairs. The teacher signaled start and stop. The winner was always given a small bar of Life Buoy soap. I was grown before I realized the same kids—the dirty ones—always got the soap. I never won.

Serious disciplinary problems among us first and second graders were handled in a long skinny room in the back called the cloak room. A summons to meet Miss Floy in this chamber of doom sent lightning bolts of horror zig zagging up and down every nerve.

In this wretched retreat she lectured longer than it took the Titanic to sink—with no hope of a lifeboat. She then applied the board of education to the seat of learning.

Her instrument of correction was a ruler. I later discovered a typical ruler is twelve inches long. The one she used was six feet and fashioned from an oak two by four . . . . with nails in it.

Few problems warranted the cloak room. Most were dispatched with a well aimed scowl that put one's heart in manic overdrive. A volume was written in that fiery glare. It echoed with hideous threats that wrought paralysis in little boys. "You'll have to stay in every recess till you're old enough to vote. One more peep out of you young man and we'll visit the cloak room."

Worse than "the eye" were her finger snaps. They could wreck a decibel meter. When her middle finger crashed into the base of her thumb a tsunami of sound engulfed the room. It flogged one's eardrums. It shook the floor. The lights reeled like the community drunk. Plaster flaked off the walls. The sonic boom knocked birds from the sky. Scruffy bare foot boys in bib overalls whimpered. On the terror scale—the cloak room being a ten—her finger snap was a six.

Seen through adult eyes Miss Floy wasn't an ogre at all. She was a dear lady, a solid citizen in the community and a gifted teacher. With meager teaching tools she bent scores of pliable lives in the direction of learning and decency.

Conscience compels me to come clean. I did win the non-musical chairs game once . . . . well, okay, more than once. I still have a bar of Life Buoy.

3

BLAZING OUTHOUSE

The mention of rabbit tobacco breaks me out in a rash; it causes me to whimper and hear killer bees buzzing behind me.

In 1950 the word macho hadn't been coined and cool had to do with temperature. Had I had those words I would have wanted to be both. I called it being grown-up. That included using tobacco.

Almost all the men in our community used tobacco. In my boyish pursuit of manliness I smoked rabbit tobacco.

Rabbit tobacco is a weed. When the leaves got dry I would chew it, smoke it in a home made corn cob pipe or roll it into cigars using newspaper. It stunk like chittlins' cooking and tasted like tainted turnips but I was lurching toward manhood so I smoked it and convinced myself that it was good.

I later learned the scientific name for rabbit tobacco is gnaphalium obtusifolium. I'm glad I didn't know that. It wouldn't sound right to ask a cohort, "wanna' hide out behind the barn and smoke some gnaphalium obtusifolium?"

Our outhouse was a perfect place to sneak a smoke. Corrugated tin served as siding on our comfort station. It had a .22 caliber bullet hole that was the right level for me to peek through to see if anyone was coming down the path. (The bullet hole was the subject of much speculation as well as some tall tales.)

One day I was smoking a fat rabbit tobacco cigar rolled in a piece of the Sunday comics when I spotted Mama coming down the path. I panicked, dropped my cigar in the hole, and ran for the woods. I made a long circuit back to the house and was playing in the dirt driveway as if nothing had happened.

But something had happened. My cigar had caught the used toilet paper on fire. When Mama stepped in the outhouse a fire was roaring in the hole. A piercing shriek echoed from the privy. She was shocked; her bladder went spastic and unburdened itself.

I saw her coming up the path with her underwear in her hand and blood in her eye. I perceived her problem pertained to me. She said, "young man you've been smoking in the toilet haven't you?" I lied like a fisherman, "no ma'am I ain't been smoking. I been out here playing". She knew better.

She ripped a limb from a privet bush, stripped the leaves off and proceeded to put my britches to blazing. Dr. Spock hadn't been heard of and timeouts hadn't been invented. All Mama knew was that a boy who sets the outhouse on fire needs a good whuppin'.

There is a difference in a spanking and a whuppin'. A spanking only hurts your feelings. A whuppin' makes you crawl up into the front of your overalls, squall, dance, writhe in agony, beg for mercy, confess your sins and make solemn promises. I would have admitted to starting the war of 1812 to get relief from the swarm of rabid bees that were loosed on my backside.

I didn't need the surgeon general to tell me that smoking was harmful to my health. I haven't smoked rabbit tobacco in fifty five years. A generation of outhouses has been spared the torch.

I never knew how Mama put out the fire in the hole. I had the curiosity but not the courage to ask.

4

MONK EYE'S MANGY MUTT

For a time, in 50s, we had neighbors with an only child, a boy my age. Everybody, including his odd parents, called him Monk Eye.

His daddy took a lot of medicine, a 90 proof concoction, made by a hermit who lived near dog river. Monk Eye said it was the only cure for his daddy's many ailments.

Had his mama, a cotton mill worker, been forced to choose between Monk Eye and her Tube Rose snuff he would have been orphaned.

One day his daddy, suffering severe sickness, went to the river recluse, and over dosed on his prescription. He clattered home in his old truck, clambered out, and staggered toward the house. He was leading a mangy three legged mutt. He slurred sloppy sentiment on Monk Eye, and presented him with "the beshst huntin' houn' in Doulash' couny. Hish' name ish' Killer." He had talked the previous owner into selling this sterling specimen of dog hood, only because the animal was gun shy.

Monk Eye started working on his new pet. He mixed a time honored cure for mange, sulphur and burned motor oil, and daubed it all over his prized pup. When he got ready to break the dog from being gun shy he called on my expertise.

In fifth grade science, at Bill Arp school, Mrs. Eunice Rice had taught us about a famous Russian named Ivan Pavlov. Mr. Pavlov conditioned dogs to salivate, at the sound of a bell, in anticipation of food. (A man with nothing to do but teach dogs to slobber probably needs a hobby.) My plan was to get Killer accustomed to hearing a bell ring, giving him food, then to transition into acclimating him to gunfire. Mr Renzo Duren loaned us a cowbell and we started our training.

After a few days of expert conditioning, when we clanged the bell, the dog would come limping, lumbering and drooling. We rewarded him with a morsel of food. Step two in Killer's training was to associate gunfire with the bell and food, then phase out the bell, and thus condition the dog to think of food when he heard the gun.

The only gun available to us was a double barrel 12gauge shotgun that Monk Eye's daddy kept behind the seat in his truck. He kept it loaded. He had told him to never bother the gun because something was wrong with it. While his daddy slept off the results of his medication we "borrowed" his gun. The barrels were so badly bent that we could have shot around corners with it.

We planned to ring the bell and when Killer came side-stepping toward the food, fire the gun. Monk Eye manned the gun; I had the bell and food. I rung the bell; Killer started toward us, and Monk Eye fired into the air.

The bent barrels weren't the primary problem with the shotgun. The real problem was that when one trigger was pulled both barrels fired at once. That 12 gauge kicked Monk Eye down, stomped on him, threw rocks at him, and cussed him.

Killer, forgetting that he was a leg shy of a full set, went out of sight over the hill wailing howls of horror. One neighbor reported seeing a slobber slinging torpedo tearing past his house, wailing like demons were on his tail. A mangled Monk Eye, his arm hanging limp, said, "I ain't never gonna try to teach a three laiged dog anythang agin."

5

DEAD MAN EATS A POTATO

I acquired an enviable education around the coal stove in the back of Mr. Bart Dukes' store, in Bill Arp. Lessons in heritage and history were woven into my memory by the yarn spinning gentry of Bill Arp.

One wintry afternoon I pulled my Orange Crush case up close to the stove, and listened as some of the best bards told their tales. One fellow's yarn has stuck in the folds of my brain. Its truthfulness was verified by several other tall tale tellers.

According to his story, during the 1920s, there was an illiterate family who lived across Dog river, near Phillip's mill. The family consisted of the father, the mother, and five boys. They disliked religion—and soap; but were on favorable terms with white lightning.

The old man, named Tatum, got pneumonia and died. It was traditional to have the body at home, and for someone to sit up around the clock until the funeral. The house bustled with friends bringing food, and taking turns sitting up.

On the second night of the wake the kitchen was filled with mourners. Someone had brought a jug of pop skull liquor and they were doing more drinking than eating. The deeper they got into the jug the less concerned they were about keeping company with Tatum.

Three Bill Arp fellows had gone to pay their respects. When they stepped up on the front porch they saw, through the open window, that no one was in the room with Tatum. They plotted to play a prank on the inebriated clan.

They had some baked sweet potatoes in the sack of food they had brought. It was well known that Tatum loved these delicious delicacies. The men crept through the window and sat Tatum up in his coffin. One of them took a big bite out of a potato. They positioned Tatum's arm up towards his mouth and stuck the potato in his hand.

Undetected, they crawled back out onto the porch. One of them yelled through the window, "hey brang me another tater." Nothing happened. Again, he bellowed, "some o' ya'll brang me another one o' them taters."

A big fearless neighbor, called Mountain seemed to have been the only one who heard the ruckus. He weaved into the front room to see who was hollering. He saw Tatum and let out a howl, like a wolf with his paw in a trap. He turned white as buttermilk and blasted through the kitchen like a cannon ball. Three men tackled him in the back yard and asked, "What in the world's wrong with you?"

Mountain, now stone cold sober, was shaking like a junior earthquake. He stammered, "Tatum's settin' up and he's eatin' a tater."

While the tipsy mob's attention was focused on Mountain, the Bill Arp pranksters removed the potato and placed Tatum in his original position.

One latecomer, and a newcomer to the jug, braved a look in the front room. He reported that Tatum was lying exactly as they had left him. His friends dragged Mountain in and forced him to look at the old man. They told him the liquor had made him see things. He said, "I know what I done seen and it's the devil that done it."

He became a teetotaler, joined the church, and attended every service. He often quoted the Scriptural warning *wine is a mocker, strong drink is raging, and whosoever is deceived thereby is not wise.* He never attended another wake.

6

HADACOL, THE CURE ALL

Child rearing experts are people who, never having bothered themselves with such undertakings as having children, delve deeply into telling the rest of us how to raise our kids—and some actually believe they know what they're talking about.

My parents never got around to reading any of their books, consequently they thought they were in charge of the kids—and they made me believe they were. In their ignorance they forced me to do things that I'm sure, any psychiatrist would acknowledge, warped my delicate psyche. It's a miracle I didn't become a bank robber, arsonist, or serial killer.

For instance, my parents insisted that I go to church every single, solitary, boring service, even on pretty days when common sense dictated that I stay home and play. But, we were allowed to stay home from church only when we were sick. In our house to be sick enough to miss church meant throwing up or running a high fever.

One Sunday, the lure of beautiful weather, building a hut, and romping in the woods, tugged harder than mama's insistence that I go to church. I devised a masterful scheme. I would pretend to be sick. Mama would leave me at home.

I would be outside playing before the '39 Chevrolet was out of sight.

On the Sunday morning of my misadventure I went to the table holding my stomach. "Mama, I don't want any breakfast I'm bad sick."

"You do look a little pale, I better give you some medicine and let you go back to bed." Mama had a counter plan. She kept, in our medicine cabinet, a tonic, concocted and marketed by Louisiana state senator Dudley J. LeBlanc, called Hadacol. When asked about its name LeBlanc said, "Well, I hadda' call it something!"

Hadacol contained so much alcohol (listed in the ingredients as a preservative) that the city of Northbrook, Illinois, only allowed it to be sold in liquor stores. Another mystery ingredient was called diluted acid hydrochloric, alleged to open the arteries so the other ingredients, including the "preservative", could be absorbed more quickly by the body. It sold for $1.25 for an eight ounce bottle. Mama thought it cured anything that ailed you.

She gave me two tablespoons of Hadacol. It tasted like burnt motor oil laced with a dead buzzard, and garnished with wild onions. I gagged and gasped. A volcanic river rushed over my tonsils. My innards chugged like an air compressor. My eyes watered and my nose ran. She then made me chase it with a snort of mineral oil (a demonic relative of castor oil). Now I was sick enough to stay home—but not to play.

I never again pretended to be sick. In fact I pretended to be well when I was sick. The Hadacol and mineral oil cure was worse than any disease. I believe it would cure fallen arches, falling hair, and mild cases of leprosy. If I had to choose between the disease and the cure, I'd choose leprosy. The $1.25 mama paid for that bottle of Hadacol was well spent.

That one bottle, threatening from the medicine cabinet, kept me well all the years of my childhood. Even now when I feel poorly I can remember the Hadacol and mineral oil cure and begin to perk up.

Who knows how I might have turned out if mama had spent her $1.25 on a book by a child rearing expert. I might be a bank robber, arsonist, or serial killer.

7

THE GOAT WHISPERER

Daniel Sullivan, a 19th century Irishman, devised a humane method of taming wild, vicious, and traumatized horses. The horse is to be treated with respect, gentleness, and firmness, but never violence.

The subject was amplified in Nicolas Evans' 1995 novel, *Horse Whisperer*. In 1998 the book was made into a Robert Redford movie, in which Sullivan's techniques were used. Much has now been written about this system of horse training.

However, until now, nothing has been written about gentling a goat. I write with some authority, in that, I may be the only person in the world—or even in Bill Arp—to have known and observed a goat whisperer at work.

In the 50s we had neighbors, with a boy my age. Monk Eye was lean as a greyhound and tough as a pine knot. He had been dazzled by the trained horses at the circus, and had ambitions to train one himself.

They couldn't afford a horse; his daddy was too sick to keep a job. He suffered from an ailment caused by overexposure—to a pint bottle.

One Saturday Monk Eye's daddy went careening down Big A road in his ratty old truck. He said he was going to get some medicine for his headache.

Hours later, he slid the rattletrap to a stop next to the woodpile, where Monk Eye and I were playing *king of the mountain*. In the back of the truck he had a big, bad, belligerent billy goat.

The old man got out and started blubbering, as only one afflicted with over exposure can. He squalled, "Monk Eye I know you been wantin' a hoss, but I been bad sick and ain't been able to buy you one, but I done taken the money I been saving for medicine and bought you this heah goat." The truth was he had won the goat in a poker game.

Monk Eye named the goat Gulliver. The next afternoon, I went to check on my noxious neighbor. He said, "I already got him so tame I don't have to tie him. Now, watch this I'm gonna' learn him to kneel like them circus horses."

He got on his knees in front of Gulliver, tapped him on the knee with a stick and said with authority, "kneel boy, kneel." The goat arched his neck, reared up on his hind legs, lowered his head, and assaulted Monk Eye. He butted him in the head slamming him onto his back. Dazed, he clambered to his hands and knees just as the goat executed a sneaky rear attack, skidding him onto his face. He attempted to get up again; he made it to his knees when the hostile goat walloped him in the belly, knocking the breath out of him. Gulliver gored the pitiful, pile of pulverized boy, several more times, bleated, and stalked off. School was out. Blood oozed from Monk Eye's flattop; an array of angry red blotches promised a kaleidoscope of color when the bruises ripened.

From my perch atop the truck, I recommended that he try again. He wheezed in a breath, his chin trembled and he whispered, "I ain't never gonna' try to learn' him nothin' else, cause he ain't got no sense."

Had Gulliver only known Mr. Sullivan's methods, he might have been more respectful, gentle, and less violent in training Monk Eye.

8

MONK EYE AND THE COOL CAT CAPER

Monk Eye suffered from a load of undeserved self confidence. He had a scalp full of scars from a failed training session with a belligerent billy goat; a gun shy three legged dog he was "training" was last seen rocketing down Big A road like a herd of demons was on his tail. Undaunted by historic mishaps and misadventures, the boy assumed himself to be an animal authority.

On a scalding hot August day we had been swimming in Bear Creek when we found a black tomcat lying under a pine tree. His labored breathing is all that distinguished him from a dead cat.

After a thorough examination Monk Eye declared he didn't suffer from broken bones, cuts, or abnormal animal ailments. Our friendship nearly ruptured when I said, "Monk Eye this ole' cat's a'gonna die, less jist leave him alone."

His doctoring skills had been challenged. Like Granny Clampett, he dug his heels in and declared, "they ain't a sick cat nowhere that I can't get well. I reckon I'll jist haf to show you."

"O.K. Mr. cat doctor, whut's wrong with that cat?"

"I'll tell ya zackly whut's wrong with him. He's done went and had hisself one a' them there heat strokes."

"Well if he has, they ain't nothin' ya can do about it."

"Oh yes they is."

"No they ain't."

"I bet you my pocket knife again' you'rn that I can git him well."

"Hits a bet."

Mama had threatened me with a whuppin' if she ever caught me gambling. But this wouldn't be gambling cause it was a certainty that Monk Eye couldn't revive a dead cat.

We took the cat to Monk Eye's house. His mama was working second shift at the cotton mill; his daddy was sleeping off the affects of some 90 proof cold medicine from the night before.

Monk Eye said, "I gotta git this cat cooled down." He stared at his mama's refrigerator and moved his mouth. He moved his mouth when he was engrossed in heavier than normal thinking. He muttered too. I think he was arguing with himself.

I was thinking too, "Don't thank about puttin' that cat in the refrigerator. Yore mama'll kill you grave yard dead." That is what he was thinking and that's what he did. He laid that cat out on the shelf with a half gallon of butter milk, a half pound of butter, and a pound of bologna.

"I'll jist leave him in there for 'bout an hour. He'll be alright when he gits cooled down."

We sauntered out to Mr. Renzo Duren's house; he had cut a watermelon and needed a couple of boys to help him eat it.

With our belly's full of melon, we meandered toward Monk Eye's house. As we approached we heard a horrible, hair raising scream. The screen door slammed back and his scrawny, bug eyed, wild haired daddy ricocheted across the yard, baggy boxer shorts flapping in the wind. He screeched, "they's a black devil in the ice box an' hit jumped me."

Monk Eye never admitted any knowledge of the "black devil". The resurrected cat was never seen again. His daddy believed his "medicine" had caused him to hallucinate. His mama didn't know how black hair got in the butter.

Monk Eye got my "real imitation pearl" handled pocketknife. If you get to heaven before me I'd appreciate it if you didn't feel compelled to tell mama about that gambling. I've never again bet against a dead cat.

9

JUICY FRUIT AND THE WOMEN'S MISSIONARY UNION

I am the only male who ever held membership in the WMU at Prays Mill Baptist church. I had this distinction in 1947 and 1948.

At that time the Women's Missionary Union met during the daytime in the church auditorium. There being no child care services provided I went to the meetings with my mother. If you need to know anything about WMU work in the late 40's I'm the authority.

Actually, my memories of the proceedings are fuzzy. My most robust recollection is being terminally bored. It had nothing to do with the meetings. It's just that the meetings weren't designed to hold the attention of a seven year old boy.

I devised a diversion to occupy my mind while the ladies met. I was the right size to lie in the floor on my back and explore underneath the pews. In this cozy hideaway my inventive juices flowed like lava.

WWII two was a fresh memory. I had heard horror stories of kamikaze attacks on our war ships, and thrilling accounts of brave airmen in their fighter planes, engaged in dogfights with the fanatical enemy. In the under pew heavens of Prays Mill Baptist church the bravest fighter pilot of them all pulled on his goggles and battled the enemy.

Lying on my back zig zagging back and forth I pushed my P51 Mustang straight up, dodging enemy planes and watching their smoky trails as they fell victim to my relentless guns.

In the pew bottom sky over my head I made a delectable discovery. Stuck around in various places were wads of gum. I chewed slightly used Juicy Fruit, Dentyne, Wrigley's Spearmint, and some undetectable brands. The gum became my award for bravery in battle. In my cozy world it was a chewy sort of war medal. I began to look forward to WMU day so I could continue my heroics.

Unknown to me I was about to get shot down in humiliation and be stripped of all my war decorations. I skidded my plane in under the last pew and was enjoying the adoration of my fellow aviators, along with yet another award—a jaw filled with second hand gum. When Mama saw me whacking away on the gum she snapped, "Where'd you get that gum."

I spluttered around my chew, "under the pew; there's plenty more. Do you want some?"

She didn't.

She made me eject my gum and convinced me I was doomed. The phrase that stuck with me was, "that filthy stuff is full of germs." I didn't know what germs were but they sounded worse than crazed kamikaze pilots. The lecture that followed was more frightening than all my dog fights. I brushed my teeth three times that night. When I went to bed I could feel creepy stealth germs plundering my body.

The lasting lesson learned from my WMU days is that vile things may happen to you if you chew ABC gum. I did learn, however, that the Dentyne bite and mellow Juicy fruit together makes a good chew. Try it sometime. You might want to use fresh gum—unless you can fit under a pew at Prays Mill church.

10

THE FLY CONVENTION

I started shinnying up the ladder of learning at Bill Arp school in 1946. We were dirty, but happy. We had not yet been inconvenienced with hygienic hype. In the fifth grade we studied a health book, and learned we were unsanitary. We didn't do anything about it, but at least we knew.

When I began school, we had a rest room for boys and one for girls. They were discreetly positioned behind the schoolhouse. In hot weather they were less discreet.

Our hands were always dirty. We ate our lunches with crusted hands. If anyone had mentioned germs, we would have assumed they referred to small Germans. And, because of World War II, Germans had fallen out of favor.

Some homes in Bill Arp had five rooms and a bath. Ours had five rooms and a path. Our outhouse squatted about 100 feet on one side of the house; the barn drooped about the same distance on the other side.

The flies ran shifts. One crew worked the outhouse while another labored in the barn. At shift change they congregated in the house to exchange greetings. A lot of them liked inside better than outside employment, so they transferred. We had screen doors and windows, and occasionally we opened them to let the flies out for fresh air and exercise.

Soon they would organize a fly convention in the kitchen. They had dive bombing exhibitions, nose tickling lessons, cornbread eating contests, nasty classes, and seminars on various forms of germ warfare.

Mama soon tired of the conventioneers antics. She would close the doors, and windows, and torpedo the enemy with DDT. About an hour after she sprayed, she opened the house up. Dead flies were laid out like slain soldiers. We were fly free, until a new crew hatched in the—well, hatched.

We did bathe regularly—every week. Mama would send us, one at a time, into a back room with a wash pan full of hot water, a bar of Lifebuoy soap, and a washcloth. Our instructions were to start at our head, and wash as low as possible; start at our feet, and wash as high as possible. Then wash possible.

In the Air Force I enjoyed a daily shower and began a sanitary existence. Most of my adult life has been spent in an unpolluted state.

In an interview, when he was the heavy weight boxing champion of the world, Leon Spinks, allegedly, said, "I've been poor, and I've been rich. Rich is better." My philosophy has been, I've been dirty and I've been clean. Clean is better.

Now, a different tale is told. There is a book, just published, entitled *Riddled With Life*. Marlene Zuk, a professor of biology at the University of California, Riverside, is the author. Her topics include: Why we can't possibly make ourselves sick by violating some of today's commonly accepted rules of hygiene. And she makes a believable case that our minds are positively influenced by parasites (she wasn't referring to congress).

According to her book, our immune systems fight harder in unclean surroundings, making them stronger and us healthier. She teaches that the negative aspects of the absence of germs is that people have more allergies, asthma, and diseases.

The professor may be right. Mama was exposed to unsanitary living conditions, ate fat meat, breathed second hand smoke and DDT, and lived to be 94. Could it be that now nasty is nice? It's possible.

11

FAMILY FUNERAL FUEDING

The summer I was twelve my brother and I stayed with preacher Carl and Mrs. Ludie Buice, on weekdays, while mama worked. I helped the preacher in his chicken house; he taught me to drive his 40 Ford pick up truck.

One day he got a call that there had been a death in Bill Arp. The family didn't have a preacher and Mr. J. Cowan Whitley, the undertaker, recommended preacher Buice. He invited me to go with him to the home of the deceased; and he let me drive.

Mr. Whitley had brought the body back home and placed the casket on a gurney in the living room. Preacher Buice went in a back room with the family to discuss funeral plans. He left me in the living room with the dead woman and an elderly, near deaf, neighbor man.

One of the sons had been drowning his grief in white lightning. He had a history of grieving; he grieved over ground hog day, weather changes, bad colds, and paved roads.

In the living room I was getting hoarse shouting at the neighbor in answer to his inquiry as to whose boy I was. Just before my voice rasped to a whisper, the back room door slammed open, and the drunken son staggered to the casket, squalling like a dying calf in a hailstorm. "Mama they ain't a'gonna let me sang at yore funeral, an' I'd done went an' picked out a real purty song fer ya. I'm sorry mama but I can't go to yore funeral with them hipercrit brothers and sisters o' mine."

He leaned on the casket talking to his mama and reached to hug her. The gurney tilted and I visualized mama sprawled on the floor. I grabbed the handle and was supporting the casket, the gurney, the dead woman, and the drunk man.

The feeble old neighbor hobbled to the scene of action, latched on to the casket handle and said, "ya dang fool you're gonna spill yore mama in the floor if ya don't quit this carryin' on an' let go of her." My skinny arms were shaking like a persimmon tree full of 'possums; the old man wasn't any stronger than I. We were losing mama when the preacher, hearing the ruckus, rushed to rescue us.

I attended the graveside funeral the next day with preacher Buice. He read Scripture, and spoke words of comfort to the family. The black sheep arrived late and stood in back of the small crowd. He had had a steadfast struggle striving to swill away his sorrow.

The preacher asked if anyone had anything they would like to say before the closing prayer. The tipsy tippler sloshed to the edge of the grave and slurred, "mama, I'm a'gonna sang ya' a song." He started bellowing a Tennessee Ernie Ford song, called *"Shotgun Boogie"*.

He sang, *"There it stands in the corner with the barrel so straight, I looked out the window and over the gate, the big, fat rabbits are a-jumpin' in the grass. Wait'll they hear my old shotgun blast . . . .* Then the edge of the grave crumbled and dumped the soused songster under the casket into the grave.

He wailed, "mama they done shoved me in heah an' they're a'gonna bary me too." The red faced preacher would have thrown the first shovel of dirt.

Precious Memories is more appropriate for funeralizing than *Shotgun Boogie*. I'm unaware of anyone ever falling into a grave singing it. However, *Shotgun Boogie* is a memory maker; I've never forgotten it.

12

BOLOGNA, BRITCHES AND A BRINDLED BULL DOG

My parents had a novel concept about work—they thought everyone should engage in it. I favored welfare. But, at their insistence, I got my first job in the summer of 1955. I was employed by Mr. Herbert Fouts at his water powered mill on Bear creek.

The turbine, which drove the machinery, was spun by water from a pond above the mill. When full, the pond was about 18 feet deep. Sweaty and dusty by lunch break, it was refreshing to leap off the dam into the icy waters of the mill pond. It was secluded in the woods so I would often eat my lunch sitting on the dam then go skinny dipping.

Mama had warned me not to go swimming after eating. She said I could get a cramp and drown. It occurred to me that I had never heard of a fish getting a cramp and dying after eating. In order to partially comply with mama's cramp concerns, I would eat one of my sandwiches, strip, jump in the mill pond, get dressed, then eat my other sandwich.

One day I disrobed for my swim, and wadded my britches and shirt around my last bologna sandwich. I plunged in deep, letting the cold water wash the mill dust off. I leisurely surfaced in the middle of the pond. All was right in my world, until I looked in the direction of my clothes.

A brindled bull dog had scented the sandwich, and was pawing at my clothes trying to get it. I shrieked uncomplimentary remarks at him. Pulling myself out of the water, I streaked at him threatening to hurl him off the dam.

He grabbed my wad of clothes and sprinted for the woods. I slipped my dripping feet into my brogans. With shoe strings flapping, the chase was on. The dog would run about a hundred feet, lay the bundle down and start mauling his way to the sandwich. I pummeled him with pine cones, rocks, limbs and unkind words. He was as insistent about having the sandwich as I was about getting back my clothes.

Panic clutched my mind like an eagle's claw. "What if I don't get my clothes back? I can't show up after lunch with nothing on but my shoes. Oh, Lord help me; and please don't help that thieving dog." I considered what to do if he escaped with my duds.

My plan was to plummet into the chilly water, get a cramp and never surface. I could visualize my grieving mama saying, "I told him he would get a cramp and drown if he eat before swimming and now he's went and done it."

A woman's voice sent my hammering heart to new heights of horror, "here Butch, here boy." I ripped through blackberry briars and cowered behind a bush. Peeking through it, I glimpsed the lady searching for her dog.

Butch got the sandwich, abandoned my bundle, and loped off in the direction of his owner. She got slobbery over him, kissing the top of his head, scratching his ears and telling him what a good boy he was. I prayed he would fall in the creek, get a cramp and drown. She left, unaware that a scratched up, praying, terrified, teenaged, skinny dipper was quivering nearby.

Clothed and in my right mind, I returned to work pondering safety slogans. *Britches and bologna don't go together. And don't swim after eating; you could get a cramp and die—even if fish don't.*

13

BUTTERMILK AND BOXER SHORTS

During the late 1940s and through the 1950s one Bill Arp character relished a cozy relationship with John Barleycorn. To protect the guilty we'll call him Jim. He was harmless to everyone but himself. He was well liked in the community, even when he was tipsy.

Since he didn't own a car it wasn't unusual to see him walking along highway 5. There was little traffic on the tar and gravel road then.

The Dowdas, Mr. Robert & Mrs. Eula, lived on highway 5. They had a house on the property where Dowda Farm Equipment is now located. Mrs. Eula kept a cow and sold milk and butter to neighbors.

One Saturday afternoon Mr. Robert came in Dukes' store and told of a calamity he had witnessed earlier that day involving Jim.

Jim had staggered down the road to their house to buy milk. While Mrs. Eula poured up his milk he sat on the porch and entertained Mr. Robert with his slurred stories. He got a half gallon of sweet milk and a half gallon of buttermilk in Mason jugs. With a jar of milk under each arm he bid them a thick tongued goodbye and reeled toward home.

Mr. Robert watched as Jim zigzagged up the road. He lurched one step forward and two side ways. His progress was further hampered by a battle between his britches, his belly and gravity. His slacks were slack with an earthward bias. He walked straddle legged to hold them up. That strategy worked on the forward step but his pants yielded ground on the side step. When they reached hazardous level he stopped and maneuvered each glass container down, like it was a baby. This operation took several suspenseful minutes. He hitched up his pants and wrestled the milk back into place.

Jim didn't get far until his trousers lost territory again. He stopped and the ordeal of handling the milk jugs was repeated. Mr. Robert lost count how many times this happened. In half an hour he hadn't made it to the curve at Mason Creek Rd.

When he had progressed almost to the curve he waited too long for a recovery. His slacks surrendered to gravity, slithered down and coiled around his feet. He stood there with a jug of milk under each arm. His knobby knees were white as marshmallows. His legs, skinny as soda straws, were exposed beneath billowing boxer shorts with big red polka dots. His pants lay puddled in defeat around his ankles.

Before he could regroup a pick up truck hauling a boisterous bunch of boys roared past, headed to their little league game. When the boys saw Jim standing in his red polka dotted boxers, pants crumpled on the ground, with a jug of milk under each arm, they went crazy whooping, hollering, and pointing. Jim never knew he had provided such a zany escapade for a group of boys.

There's a lesson here. Avoid alcohol lest you find yourself standing beside the highway, with a jug of milk under each arm, modeling your red polka dotted boxer shorts for a raucous little league team.

14

JIP AND THE SETTIN' HEN

The gutsiest dog I ever knew was Jip. In the early fifties he was the undefeated general on our end of King's highway. I loved that twelve pounds of dynamite. He was part feist, fox terrier, unknown and Tasmanian devil—he was all bad.

Jip was loving and loyal to our family. He disliked the rest of the world except for our cats Tom and Jerry—both female. They shared his bed and feed bowl.

Jip was our protector. He challenged everything and everybody who braved our yard. He was no respecter of persons; he once bit our pastor.

Jip loved rambling in the fields and woods. The brown torpedo stumbled over more rabbits than a Beagle could jump on purpose. He had superman vision and could spot a squirrel in the highest reaches of a poplar tree. You knew when he treed one. The worse thing about Jip was his voice. It sounded like a hyena gargling—with turpentine.

He patrolled the perimeter of the yard like he was guarding fort Knox. We had about two dozen free ranging Bantams. Jip didn't allow them in the yard.

It was common for the Bantam hens to lay their eggs in the woods where we couldn't find them. They would then set on them for three weeks and hatch out babies. We called them settin' hens. I was never sure of the proper grammar. I didn't know whether to call them settin' hens or sittin' hens. Our concern was when they cackled were they layin' or lyin'.

One day a little hen came into the yard followed by five biddies. Jip was on patrol. He spotted them. "Not in my yard," the torpedo said. "You and your little fuzz balls better head for the woods." Traveling at the speed of light he broke the sound barrier hurtling toward the little mother and her brood. His legs pumped so fast they looked like wheels skimming the ground.

However, there was an occurrence outside the realm of Jip's experience. The little hen didn't run. She dropped her wings and when the blur came in reach pounced on his head. Protective wings and beak machine gunned his head and back like a swarm of rabid bees. The hyena screamed as he catapulted toward the house. "Braarp, braarp, braarp," and he meant it.

The house sat about eighteen inches off the ground and wasn't underpinned. His head hit every floor joist until he was ensconced deep under the house behind the chimney foundation. There he lay whimpering, pondering and wondering if a dog could join the Foreign Legion. Life, as he knew it, had ended like a bad movie.

Now when any chicken came in the yard Jip found urgent business down at the barn. Jip's defeat was a victory for all the bantams. Every Napoleon has his Waterloo. Jip's was a Bantam settin' hen. Jip never chased another chicken. He still chased cars. One day he caught one. Fifty odd years later I still miss him and his rascality. He was like any other dog—but more so.

15

BUSTER, BEES, AND BRUTON

In all my 12 years I had never known as mischievous a menace as Monk Eye. Something, usually catastrophic, happened when my neighbor was involved.

One such venture began when Monk Eye traded a billy goat for a dog named Buster. The dog had spindly Rat Terrier like legs, the coloring of a Blue Tick hound, and he had some Dachshund length to him. One ear bent down and one pointed up. He had a semi-bulldog face, and the deep bark of a Bassett hound. The F.B.I. could not have traced his ancestry.

One cold blustery night Monk Eye and I went to the woods to catch a 'possum or two. His mama would pay us 50 cents each for them. We took a three cell flash light, my Red Ryder B.B. gun, a burlap bag to carry the 'possums in, and Buster.

After half an hour of rambling through the woods Basset voiced Buster struck a trail. He led us to a sweet gum tree. We spotted the 'possum out on a bottom limb about 15 feet above us. Buster was pawing and gnawing the tree. His excited basset bark was reduced to a snuffling sound, like a hog in distress.

Our plan was for one of us to climb the tree and shake the 'possum out; the dog would catch it; and we would take it away from the dog. I let him persuade me to stay on the ground while he climbed the tree to shake the 'possum out. He shinnied up the tree and found a knot hole well situated to put his foot in and support himself while he shook the 'possum out.

He began shaking the limb and yelling at the 'possum. "Jump 'possum, jump. Ya ain't afraid a' ol' Buster are ya?" He hollered and yelled and shook. Buster, anxious for action, was frenzied, and trying to climb the tree.

Monk Eye's banshee screaming became frantic and reached new notches on the decibel scale. He was in dire distress. The knot hole was the front door for a colony of honey bees. He was covered with crawling bees before he knew he was in trouble. As if on cue they seemed to all begin stinging at once. He was squalling and clambering out on the 'possum limb. "Hep' me, please hep' me."

I said, "Monk Eye they ain't no way fer me to hep' ya." I had compassion for him—but not enough to get mixed up with those bees.

"Go get Mama to come hep' me. I'm 'agonna die up heah. Hep' me Lord an' I won't cuss no more, never". Slapping bees with both hands he lost his balance and came crashing down. Kawhump, It sounded like an elephant hitting the ground. I thought he was dead. Bees by the dozen were humped up on him pumping their venom into his hide. Buster, assuming the world's biggest 'possum had just hit the ground, attacked Monk Eye. I began smacking the dog with the flash light, and trying to decide how I could tell Monk Eye's mama that he was dead.

Then I heard him capture a breath. He livened up fast, stripped off his bee infested clothes, and headed for home and relief. His mama daubed 57 stings with Bruton snuff. He looked like a Dalmatian puppy.

Monk Eye resumed cussing, quit 'possum hunting, and traded Buster to the rolling store man for a crippled duck. It was a good swap. Ducks have never been known to tree a 'possum in a bee tree.

16

THE RED ROOSTER THE ROLLING STORE AND THE RED MAN

Every Tuesday the rolling store man rattled down Kings Highway. A modified school bus was his store. A crate of live chickens was wired to the back. He carried the basic groceries that country folks needed. Things like Spam, Vienna sausages, potted meat, pork and beans, and saltines graced his shelves. Drinks were iced down in an old cooler bolted to the floor.

He was tall, spare framed, with a squared off Dick Tracy face. He wore Lee overalls, a battered felt hat, and he chewed tobacco. If tobacco chewing is an art form, his name was Rembrandt. He painted a picture of contentment, satisfaction, and intelligence with his expert manuvering of his cud. The way he wallowed it around in his cheek, his raptourous expression, and his accurate spitting, was a wonder for a nine year old boy to behold. I longed to chew tobacco—just like this artist.

We had a massive, mean rooster of the Rhode Island Red persuasion. With no provocation, apart from satanic influence, he often attacked me. I hated him.

One Tuesday mama had gone to the field to call papa [my granddaddy] to dinner. She left me some money and a list of items to buy if the rolling store came while she was gone. He came and I got the few groceries she wanted.

He asked if we had any chickens to sell. I fibbed, "my granddaddy's got a big red rooster he wants to sell."

"Do you know how much he wants for the rooster?"

I lied again, "Yessir, he said he'd take an RC Cola, a Moon pie, a Hershey bar and a pack of Red Man chewing tobacco."

"Fair enough." The deal was done. Dick Tracy cornered and crated the rooster, and the rolling store careened down the road.

Swaying in the porch swing I scarffed down the Hershey bar and Moon pie like a hungry hobo, and washed them down with ice cold RC Cola. Now it was time for dessert.

I wrestled a wad of Red Man into my jaw. Rembrandt was a no show; I didn't even make the paint by number level of the art of chewing. Half cleaned chitlins' soaked in turpentine and burned motor oil would have been an improvement. I kept chewing, thinking it would get better. It didn't. I spit it out—too late.

I got queasy. The world was spinning, stars were flashing and falling, roman candles were firing inside my head. Sweating and gagging, I made it into the yard where the Hershey bar made an explosive re-appearance, and my nose squirted RC foam; the Moon pie went into eclipse. My legs were weak and wobbly. I staggered, gyrated, heaved, and moaned; my innards percolated like a coffee pot.

Mama and papa came into the yard and saw my suffering. Mama asked, "What in the world's wrong with you?"

Papa said, "If I had a dog carryin' on like that I'd worm him."

I got into the house and onto the twisting, bucking couch. Mama thought I had one of the new viruses going around. I knew the name of this one, but she would never know.

I survived the virus, and developed a bad attitude toward the rolling store and Dick Tracy. I suggested that a fox might have eaten the rooster.

That was a good chew. Nearly 60 years later I've never needed another one. And, I've never had worms.

17

PAINTED PIG'S FEET

New York Yankee's pitcher, Don Larson, made sports history on October 8, 1956 pitching the only perfect game in world series history. It was the fifth game of the contest against the Brooklyn Dodgers. After the no-hitter a mentally challenged sports reporter asked manager, Casey Stengel, if that was the best game Larson had ever pitched. Stengel's tongue in cheek, answer was, "so far." The game's most memorable picture was catcher, Yogi Berra, leaping into Larson's arms after the 27th out.

In that same year, hog history happened here. The brain dead reporter could have rescued his ragged reputation but, alas, that journalist, nor any other, was on hand when Susie, my thoroughbred Spotted Poland China pig, won a blue ribbon at the Coosa Valley fair, in Rome, GA.

I became a sow specialist through the teaching of Mr. Frank Cloer, our agriculture teacher. He encouraged me to work with Susie daily, from the time she was eight weeks old, preparing her for the show ring. When Mr. Cloer declared Susie ready, so was I.

On the appointed day we went to the fair. Each hog in her category was assigned a small pen with a thick carpet of shavings on the floor, and access to a water hose for bathing (the hog not the boy).

A dirty pig could be disqualified. I washed my hog; her skin glistened through the bristles. Her hooves had to be clean and shiny; that had concerned me. Even hard scrubbing with soapy water never made them shine. Once, at home, I had used Mama's clear finger nail polish on Susie's feet and made them sparkle; I smuggled a bottle into her pen.

As show time closed in I gave Susie a final bath, and painted her hooves. A farmer, whose son had a pig in the show, was sauntering through the pig barn admiring the animals. Down on one knee examining Susie, he asked, "how'd you get them hooves so shiny?" With the confidence of an expert hogologist, I told him my secret for the well groomed hog. He said, "son them judges will disqualify your pig when they see her hooves."

My group had been notified to be ready to enter the show ring in 30 minutes. Panicked, I flitted about asking every woman I could find, "Ma'am could I borrow some nail polish remover?" They gave the deranged 15 year old eye rolling looks that said, "this young generation's going to the hogs."

Finally, a grandmotherly lady asked, "why in the world do you want nail polish remover?" When I explained, this angelic woman said, "come on we ain't got much time." She crawled in the pen with me and we went to work unpolishing Susie's hooves. She was finishing the last toenail when my name was called.

Pretty, proud, and perky, like any beauty contestant, Susie promenaded before the judges. Recognizing hog superiority, they awarded her the blue ribbon.

Don Larson's no hitter has its place in sports history; but if there was a hog world series, as there should be, Susie would be in the hall of fame. Where is a reporter when history is being made? Probably, asking dimwitted questions at a lesser event.

Mrs. White, the lady who saved my bacon, so to speak, came by our pen. She gave Susie an apple core and me a bear hug, saying, "See hon you don't have to cheat to win."

"Yes ma'am, I've shore learned my lesson, thank you for hepin' me," I responded to the judge's wife.

18

MONK EYE AND THE DRIVERLESS TRUCK

Monk Eye's most catastrophic escapade involved his daddy's truck, a vehicle of questionable ancestry. The fenders flopped, the tailgate flapped, the windshield was cracked, the doors rattled, the tires were maypops, and the muffler had a hole in it. If you rolled it down hill and popped the clutch—and were lucky—it might start.

On the disastrous day of Monk Eye's near demise he went to Douglasville with his daddy. He left the old truck idling while he went in the cotton mill to pick up his wife's pay; Monk Eye stayed in the truck.

His imagination painted pretend pictures. He crawled under the steering wheel of the ancient truck. He was a cop chasing dangerous, desperate, gangsters. He toed the shiny accelerator pedal, like he'd seen his daddy do. The aged engine revved but the truck didn't go. He squashed it harder; the motor roared; the truck still didn't move. He knew his daddy did something with the lever in the floor; he jerked it with all his 10 year old might.

There was gear box grinding and transmission turmoil; the bellowing truck, spewed gravel from its rear wheels, and lurched across the parking lot. Panicked, Monk Eye stiffened thus smashing the accelerator harder. The truck bolted, side swiped a late model Hudson, slid sideways and careened toward the edge of the parking area.

Joe, an unemployed local legendary drinker, staggered across the field adjacent to the parking lot. The fiendish truck, appearing to be driverless, abandoned the parking lot, roared across the field, and hurtled toward Joe. Suddenly sober, he speedily sought safety behind an oak tree.

Terrified, Monk Eye bailed out. He used the steering wheel for leverage, which redirected the truck; it slammed into Joe's sanctuary. The headlights wrapped around the tree like a cross eyed monster; the radiator whished out a geyser of steam; the engine died; Joe got serious about staying sober.

People from the mill ran to investigate. Joe told them, "Thet old truck come a'tearin down through heah and plumb run over thet there boy layin' over yonder. I seed the whole thang. Hit woulda' got me if'n I hadn't a jumped behind thet tree. An' they weren't nobody a'drivin' it."

Monk Eye had been scratched, but not hurt plunging from the truck. Overhearing Joe's version of the events, he was quick to recognize an opportunity to save himself from his daddy's wrath. He lay still as a dead 'possum. A man came to check on him. The victim groaned. The good Samaritan shouted, "he's alive but he's bad hurt."

His mama ran from the cotton mill squalling, "my pore young'un's done went and got hisself kilt." She fell on him howling, "speak to me baby."

Monk Eye eased out of his counterfeit coma. "Wha' happened?"

She said, "sompin' done went and happened to yore daddy's old truck and thet thang run over you."

Monk Eye was treated like a war hero. He regaled one and all about how he was just throwing gravel at the oak tree; he heard a noise and turned to see the driver less truck zeroed in on him . . . and then everything went black. Drunk or sober, his daddy never figured out what happened that day.

Monk Eye and I were eating candy, brought to him by a neighbor to speed his recovery, when he told me the true version of his escapade. We agreed it would hurt Joe's feelings if folks learned he didn't really see what he saw . . . and they would quit bringing candy.

19

THE CHRISTMAS PONY

His breath singed my hair; curled my toenails and caused my eyes to water. When he said Ho, Ho, Ho, crime scene tape had to be strung. Last year, Santa had blue eyes and peppermint breath. This year he had bloodshot brown eyes and gangrene breath.

With a tornado of toxic fumes swirling around my head, it was difficult to gag out my request. I willed my adenoids to rise in the back of my throat and seal off my nostrils. This caused me to have a notable nasal twang. When I said, "I need a pony", he thought I said his knees were bony, and got huffy. You don't want sewer breath Santa huffing in your direction.

I was there to plead for a pony. Johnny Mack Brown, Gene Autrey, and Roy Rogers all had horses. I fantasized about being a cowboy like them. I needed a pony.

My grandfather said I shouldn't expect a pony because I didn't know how to ride one if I got it. He agreed to help remedy this shameful shortage of skill. Papa tied a rope around Buck, a bony bull yearling that Daddy had. He dragged him up next to a stump. I climbed on the stump and clambered aboard the calf. I felt like a real cowboy. From the dizzy height of three and a half feet I looked down on the pitiful pedestrian world. Buck didn't share my enthusiasm. I bumped him in the ribs with my imaginary spurs. I clucked and kicked to no avail.

Papa said, "I'll make him move". He flailed the bull with his hat and let out a war whoop like Geronimo. Buck developed an uncivil opinion toward my cowboy education. He fired off like a bullet. In one tenth of a second he rocketed to ninety three MPH, and zeroed in on the barbed wire fence like a heat seeking missile.

I had a vice grip on the rope. My body hung out over the bull's back snapping like a flag in the wind. When Buck was approximately one sixteenth of an inch from the fence he stopped; I didn't. I did a somersault over the fence, made a one point landing on my back and bounced to a stop, cuddling a pine sapling. Enough wind was knocked out of me to float the Goodyear blimp. I couldn't pull any air into my lungs.

Contrary to what you may have heard, a dying person doesn't see beautiful lights and hear soothing heavenly anthems. One sees a kaleidoscope of horror cascading around him. A barbed wire fence approaching at warp speed; a mangled body; Papa screaming, "don't spur him," and a murder minded bull gloating and thumbing his nose at you. Then, you do hear music—funeral music.

Teeter tottering on the brim of a black hole I managed to suck in a humming bird breath. Dazed, I staggered back from the brink and reassembled my bleeding body parts. Papa shook his head and said, "you shouldn't have spurred him."

Dear Santa,
 Don't bring me a pony. Papa's done talked me out of being a cowboy. I'm gonna be a doctor. Please bring me a doctor's kit—with lots of band aids.

Instead of cookies and milk I'll leave a bowl of peppermints. Please help yourself. Get enough for next year too.

Thank you for not bringing me a pony.

20

THE CHITLIN' CHALLENGE

Hog killing had to be done on a cold day. One freezing morning I was awakened with the declaration, "get up we're killing hogs today."

The hog was slaughtered, hung by its hind feet, scalded, the hair scraped off, and gutted. The intestines were dumped into a wheelbarrow. My assignment was to haul them to the back woods and bury them.

We had a neighbor whose life had three cycles, getting drunk, sleeping off a drunk, and being hung over from a drunk. His wife worked at the cotton mill in Douglasville. Monk Eye, their only child, was left to fend for himself, which meant he rarely attended school.

On this hog killing day Monk Eye wandered down to our house, and watched the proceedings. As I prepared to haul off the innards he said, "Daddy likes chitlins'. Can he have a mess?"

Papa said, "he kin have 'em all if he wants 'em." Monk Eye ran home, aroused his daddy from a 90 proof nightmare, and inquired if he would like some chitlins'.

He slurred, "I wouldn't mind a good mess o' chitlins', an' some brains too, them's good scrambled with aigs."

Papa split open the hog's skull, scooped out the brains, and put them in a small bucket. He told us to take Monk Eye's daddy a mess of chitlins' and the brains.

I didn't know what part of the hog's sewage system was used for chitlins', nor was I sure how much a "mess" was. Monk Eye and I hauled the whole wheelbarrow to his house; we wanted to make sure the old man had enough for a mess.

He awakened his daddy again to ask him where to put his "mess" of chitlins'. The old man mumbled, "put 'em on the porch 'an I'll fix 'em atter I git to feelin' better."

So we dumped the animal's septic tank and drain field on the porch near the door. "That a'way they'll be handy for daddy to find when he gets ready to fix 'em", Monk Eye said.

Just before dark I was milking Gurney, our little cow, when I heard a shrill voice screeching down across the barnyard. I peeked around the corner of the barn and saw Monk Eye's mama. She had the boy backed up against the house, shaking her finger in his face.

She had come home from work, and discovered the porch decorated with a monstrous mess of oozing, putrid, porker parts. She had shaken the old man awake and asked, "what in the world's that pile o' guts doin' on the porch?" He muttered that Monk Eye had gotten them a mess of chitlins'. She found Monk Eye at our house.

She did some first class, innovative, artistic, oratorical cussing. She used double-jointed, compounded cuss words. In her foaming fury she freckled the boy with Tube Rose snuff. The hog killing crew watched in awe, like storm chasers who are finally seeing the tornado of the century. I prayed for Monk Eye's survival; I prayed she wouldn't learn that I had a part in the chitlin' caper—so far she hasn't.

Her cussing sputtered to a crash landing, but not before she told Monk Eye, "them hog guts better be gone afore dark or you'll be in real bad trouble." If this wasn't real bad trouble I couldn't bear to see it.

After she stormed off I said, "you may want to save that bucket of brains." He didn't. In a neighborly gesture I offered to let him borrow our wheelbarrow.

21

A WELL, A BELL, AND UNCLE DELL

I once heard an old man tell a tall tale about a happening near the Winston community. It occurred, according to him, in the early 1900s, and involved an old farmer, whom everyone called uncle Dell. His wife's name was aunt Mattie.

Aunt Mattie was a devout Christian, but uncle Dell didn't believe in prayer, never read the Bible, and rarely attended church. Aunt Mattie said he was a 'heathern'. One friend said, "religion to ol' Dell is like a small pox vaccination, he's got jist enough exposure to keep him from ketchin' it".

Uncle Dell was fond of Kate, a little white mule he had plowed for over 20 years. She had gone blind, and could no longer work; but he kept her for sentiments sake. He put a bell around her neck to keep up with her in the pasture.

A rat had gotten into uncle Dell's well and fouled the water. He prepared to go down in the well to fish out the dead varmint. He removed the well curb, tied a rope to a nearby tree, got a bucket to dip up the rancid rodent, and lowered himself into the well.

A neighbor, a fellow named Jess, sauntered up and saw that uncle Dell was in the well. Jess was in the final stages of inebriation, and full of devilment. The circumstances were ripe for prank pulling.

He went to the pasture, took the bell off Kate and strolled toward the well, ringing it. Uncle Dell thought Kate was out of the pasture. He hollered for aunt Mattie, but she didn't hear him.

The tingling got closer; uncle Dell had a vivid vision of him and the mule in close fellowship in the bottom of the well. As the bell came nearer he began talking to Kate, "Gee, [turn right] Kate, gee." The jangling was closer. He yelled louder, "Haw, [turn left] Kate, haw. The clanging kept coming. Edging toward panic he wailed, "Whoa Kate, whoa girl, back up Kate, back up now girl." The demonic dingdong of doomsday was closing in.

Desperate, he prayed, "Lord hep me. Please don't let Kate fall in heah on me." She seemed but steps away now. "Lord Kate ain't a'mindin' me, maybe if'n you spoke to her she'd stop." The gonging approached the edge of the well; plaintive praying echoed from deep down. "Lord, I'm a'gonna' believe the Bible jus' like Mattie does, and if'n you'll stop thet mule I'll read it ever day, an' pray, and go to Sunday meetin' reglar."

The death knell began to fade away from the well. Jess had replaced the bell, and staggered toward home before uncle Dell's shattered nerves settled enough for him to climb out. Shaken and shuddering, he teetered into the house.

"Did you git the rat?" Aunt Mattie asked.

He gasped, "I shore did, and thet ain't all, I got religion down in thet well."

"Don't be a heathern, you can't git religion in a well."

"Hit ain't easy fer me to tell about, and hit ain't easy fer me to forgit about. I jist know the Lord shore 'nuff answers prayer, an' you'll see me a'doin' a heap of it from now on, an' I'll be a'goin' to meetin' with you too"

The Lord used a dead rat, a drunk, and a bell to get a 'heathern' to make prayers and promises.

22

TEARING DOWN THE OLD OUTHOUSE

One sizzling summer day during dog days of 1951 I rode my bike to Dukes' store in Bill Arp. Mama sent me to get a can of Spam and a box of saltine crackers, and gave me a dime to spend on myself. I got two drinks, a Nehi strawberry and an Orange Crush and proceeded to guzzle them.

An old man, who was a regular at the store, sauntered in, got himself a dope (that's what old timers called Cokes) and a pack of peanuts. He plopped down on the drink box, dangled his feet, poured the peanuts in his Coke, and began telling tall tales about Bill Arp. One of them has stuck in my mind until I can quote it almost like he told it.

He said a soldier returned to the Bill Arp family farm after WWI. The first morning home he asked his daddy if there was anything he could do to help out. His daddy said, "well the only thing I had planned for today was to tear down the old outhouse. I've built us a new one."

"Papa, let me do it. I'll show you what I've learned in the army."

"Well alright if that's what you want to do."

The army had trained the soldier in explosives and demolition. He got a half stick of dynamite from the tool shed, where his daddy kept it for blowing stumps out of the ground.

He attached a cap and fuse in the end of the dynamite. "Watch this Papa." He shoved it up under the old outhouse, lit the fuse, and he and his daddy ran behind the smoke house. KABLOOM! The old privy splintered into a thousand pieces.

"How's that for making short work of a job Papa?"

"The army shore knows how to get things done don't they?"

Later that morning the young man was helping his daddy shuck some corn. His mother, came down to the corn crib. "Have ya'll seen grandpa? I can't find him anywhere."

They started looking and the more they looked the more concerned they became. Suddenly she clapped her hand over her mouth, sucked in a great gulp of air and said, "oh my goodness, grandpa never would use the new toilet. You don't suppose . . . oh I can't even think about it."

They hurried to the scene of destruction and started pawing through the shattered debris. About 20 feet from the site they found grandpa entangled in blackberry brambles. His clothes were tattered, his hat was battered, and he was scratched up like he had been the referee in a cat fight.

He was stunned speechless and pale as a catfish's belly. They got the dazed old man to the house, laid him on a bed, and bathed his face with cold water. Grandpa began coming out of his fog. He sat up, blinked his eyes, shook his head and said, "by George, that's the last time I'll light my pipe in the outhouse."

His tale told, and his dope finished, the old timer ambled out of the store and down the road. I still don't know if it was true or if a wide-eyed country boy got his leg pulled; I lean toward the latter.

It does, however, illustrate that smoking is bad for your health—especially if you light up in . . . the wrong place.

23

MONK EYE'S MONSTER MACHINE MISHAP

In 1934 the first Soap Box Derby, the copyrighted idea of newsman Myron Scott, was held in Dayton, Ohio. The next year it was moved to Akron, Ohio where the World Championship finals have been held each August since.

The races have divisions to accommodate youngsters from ages 8-17. The racers are built low to the ground, have weight limitations and their only power is the downhill pull of gravity. The wheels must be regulation soapbox derby wheels. The little cars sometimes reach speeds of 35 miles per hour.

My soapbox experience took place on Kings Highway, when it had ditches on each side, and hadn't been violated by pavement. Daddy bought my brother and me an official set of soapbox derby racing wheels. We built our car from scrap lumber, and a scavenged steering wheel from a junked model A Ford.

The steering wheel was attached to a rod (a whittled down length of dogwood). A one quarter inch cable was wound around the steering rod and fastened to each end of the front axle, which was attached to a pivoting stabilizer. When the steering wheel was turned the cable took up slack on one end of the axel and let it out on the other end thus turning the wheels and guiding the car.

We discovered that by winding the cable backwards on the steering rod the wheels would turn in the opposite direction from which the steering wheel was turned. To go left you turned right; to go right you steered left. We honed our skill in backward steering.

One day my nimble neighbor nuisance, Monk eye, rattled up on his rickety bike as I flashed down the hill on the miniature monster machine. There was nothing Monk Eye wouldn't attempt; and he bore trophy scars from his near fatal feats. He said, "hey lemme ride that little old thang.

I said, "Monk Eye, that soap box is kinda' tricky, you might not be able to drive it."

That hurt his feelings. He said, "Git it up to the top of the hill and gimme' a good push an' I'll show you I kin drive." We pushed it to the top of the hill; he got situated on the seat and yelled, "now gimme' a good shove." I did, but didn't tell him about the steering system surprise.

The soap box sped down the hill for about 50 feet before drifting toward the ditch. Monk Eye turned the steering wheel away from the ditch, which of course, slammed him into it.

"Monk Eye, I thought you said you could drive."

"I kin drive. I dunno' what happened. Lemme try it agin'."

He tried it again. This time the little vehicle careened down the hill for about 75 feet before it got a hankering to fellowship with a deep ditch. He snatched the wheel away from the ditch. Kawham! The speedster smashed into a red clay bank catapulting Monk Eye flailing skyward like a wounded goose. He crash landed in a briar patch.

I extracted my racer from the ditch; it had fared far better than Monk Eye.

Dazed from the wreck and defiled by the briars he clambered out into the road.

I said, "I guess you just ain't got the hang of driving," and shoved off, hurtling down the road.

I pushed it back to the top of the hill. "Come on Monk Eye, try it again."

Blood, tears, and defeat dripped down his chin. "Naw, I ain't a gittin' on that #%@&* thang agin. I ain't old enough to drive nohow."

24

JAKE THE SNAKE AIN'T JAKE

King snakes are beneficial. They are harmless, eat rodents, and kill poisonous snakes. Some of the farmers used to put them in their barns, or corncribs, to control rats. Papa, my mama's daddy, brought one home to guard our crib. He named him Jake.

Papa lectured us on the advantages of having the reptilian rattrap. He warned that dire consequences would befall any person who harmed Jake. So began a sad saga that would end in merciless murder.

Mama's opinion was that a good snake was one that had some distance between his head and body. She said, "I'd rather have a wheel barrow full of rats than to have a snake." When papa would brag on Jake's efficiency, mama, always behind his back, would make vigorous chopping motions with an imaginary hoe. Women folks aren't snake friendly—even with friendly snakes.

From time to time I would spy Jake lounging in the crib, often with a rat sized belly bulge. He maintained the same address for about two years, and developed into a shiny, beautiful animal.

In the spring of 1952 papa went on vacation with one of his sons. His parting instructions to me were to keep fresh water out for Jake, and not let anything happen to him.

A few days after papa left I was shucking corn, but not fast enough to suit mama. She came to check on my progress, or lack thereof. She brought a hoe with her. "Just in case," she said.

We were almost finished with the scratchy, itchy job when I spotted Jake sliding across a partition that separated the crib into two sections. I began to pray that mama wouldn't see him. The Lord didn't smile on Jake.

Mama let out a squall like a mad moose and grabbed the hoe. This weapon of war proved more deadly than a heat-seeking missile. Jake was at a distinct disadvantage. His only defense was—well he didn't have a defense. He stared at me with unblinking eyes as if to say, "papa said for you to protect me." But I knew I was no match for a frenzied female armed for Armageddon. I opted for self-preservation, abandoned Jake, and shamefully turned away. The hoe sounded like a stuttering machine gun. Small flying snake parts peppered me.

I collected the remnants of Jake's remains and buried them in the garden. Mama said, "now there's a good snake for you." She made veiled threats as to what would happen to a boy who ratted on her about killing the rat killer.

Papa returned from his vacation and, before he set his suitcase down, asked about Jake. I said, "I ain't seen Jake but once since you left." I saw no reason to tell him that he had been filleted into tiny bloody pieces when I last saw him.

After several days of fretting about what could have happened to his pet, he came in one day and announced, "now I know what happened to Jake." Mama froze over the dough board, where she was making biscuits. My heart began to jack hammer. I developed ill feelings toward our dog, assuming she had dug up the mangled corpse.

Papa said, "I found a nest in the crib with 10 or 12 baby snakes hatching out. Jake was a female; she laid her eggs and left. We'll have plenty of king snakes now." Mama looked faint and appeared to be on the outskirts of a nervous breakdown. Jake was a gender bender who was really Jane.

25

PAPA'S PLUMP PUNGENT POSSUM

Mama's widowed daddy, Papa Jones, lived with us most of my childhood. He farmed, chopped wood, told hair raising ghost stories, and talked about the "good ole' days".

One night, reminiscing about raising his family during the depression, he told how rabbits and squirrels provided their meat, along with an occasional 'possum. He would fatten this dinner delicacy on cornbread for three weeks, then prepare it for a big Sunday meal. He got glassy eyed telling how the family gathered around and dined on a tasty fat 'possum.

Mama, too, had memories of those days and dinners; hers weren't pleasant. She said, "I'll starve to death before I take another bite of 'possum. It's greasy, stringy, and stinks worse than 'chitlins cooking in collards. 'Possums are cousins to buzzards. Better not anybody ever bring one of them scavengers in my house."

Unbeknownst to Mama, Papa caught a 'possum and put it in a rabbit hutch. He began smuggling left over cornbread to the 'possum pen.

One day he said to me, "my 'possum's about ready to eat. The first time yore Ma goes off fer a day I'll show you what good eatin' is."

In a few days Mama visited her sister in Atlanta. Papa and I were left alone for the day, the poor 'possum's last day.

We prepared the animal. Papa said, "take them guts and skin and bury 'em in the woods. Thata' way yore Ma won't ever know about our 'possum." I don't know when it became "our" 'possum, but it looked like I was now locked into this criminal caper.

Papa began cooking the skinned dog look alike in Mama's oven in a shallow pan. Every few minutes he'd take a spoon and dip up the grease that was cooking out of the 'possum. He said, "keeping the grease dipped off is the secret to fixin' a good 'possum."

Outside our dog, Jip, began yelping like Hitler, Mussolini, and Jack the ripper had all stopped by. Pat and Kate, our mules, had gotten out and were sauntering around, exploring the yard.

If the Olympics had a cussin' event, Papa would have snagged the gold. He limbered up, charging after the mules, flinging red hot, double barreled expletives at them. He succeeded in chasing them into the woods. He cussed the mules, the pasture fence, the woods, bad luck, his hernia, and then he cussed cause he had some never deployed cuss words. Left over cuss words ricocheted off rocks and trees, and fluttered past me like spent bullets.

After hours of mule chasing, Pat and Kate went back into the pasture across the downed fence where they had escaped. We repaired the fence and trudged home.

Before we reached the house we were assaulted by a pungent, burnt motor oil, leaky septic tank smell. Our forgotten dinner was now a charcoal 'possum. His fragrance permeated the house. The stove needed crime scene tape around it. Papa needed cardiac care.

Near time for Mama to come home Papa got an itch to go for a long walk. He said, "you explain to your Ma what happened to our 'possum. Maybe she won't get too mad at you." Somehow I had acquired a share in the 'possum and a share in the punishment.

I met Mama at the car. She said, "good grief, what's that awful smell?"

I made a full confession. I said, "Papa burnt his 'possum in your oven."

In no more than a week Mama resumed speaking to him—on a limited basis.

His craving cured, Papa never caught, kept, or cooked another 'possum.

26

THE BULL DOG AND THE DUMB BULL

The year before my arrival on the planet, my granddaddy [papa] and my uncle [Willard] plotted against four boys. Their plan involved an instrument of insanity called a dumb bull.

This Halloween horror is made with a short section of hollow log, or a small nail keg. A raw hide is stretched over one end and secured, making a drum like apparatus. A heavy cord is threaded into the center of the hide from inside the log, and knotted on the outside. Beeswax is applied to the cord. When the master of mischief reaches inside the log, grips the cord, and slides his hand down the string, it produces an indescribable growl that can be altered according to the operator's expertise.

On a full moon night Willard organized a 'possum hunt with his friends. One boy, Preston, owned a bulldog named Pug. The dog, according to his boastful owner, was afraid on nothing.

Papa was sitting by the fire chewing tobacco, and reading a week old Atlanta Constitution when the nocturnal nimrods, and their dogs, assembled for their outing. The jovial juveniles made for the woods. Papa took the dumb bull, cut across a field, and positioned himself on a hillside near where the fearless foursome was going.

Tramping along, Willard told lies about a crazed animal that had been sighted in these woods. He told terrifying tales of neighbors who had heard its unearthly roar. He said one farmer had lost a yearling to it. It had killed a hog on another farm. Tracks, as big as a man's hat, had been found.

Preston said, "they ain't nothin' livin' that'll bother us long as we got 'ol Pug. He'd whup that thang and tare 'im up like he wuz a slab o' fatback."

The dogs struck a trail and treed a 'possum. Lanterns bobbed as the boys gathered around a Poplar tree. The frenzied dogs were yelping, yipping, baying and barking. The pugilistic Pug was biting and pawing the tree.

In the midst of this tsunami of sound Papa cut loose with a big bellow from the dumb bull. Willard asked, "did ya'll hear that? Listen."

With an eerie, vibrating, moaning, bass sound the dumb bull roared again. Willard said, "that must be that thing that's been killing livestock around here."

The dogs quit barking on the next blast, tucked their tails and sidled up next to their boy. Pug whimpered like a scared pup. Willard fired their fear, "it sounds like he's headed this way."

An angry, roaring lion sound, rumbled down the hill. Willard yelled, "run, here it comes." Wild, snuffling noises echoed toward the sprinting boys. Pug released a frantic, quivery yelp, passed the fleeing fellows, and led the pack in their frantic flight.

A slower boy grabbed the coattail of a passing buddy. He screamed, "don't leave me fellers, that thang's got aholt o' me." They left him.

Papa hurried back across the field and was sitting by the fire when the boys thundered into the house. The dogs, led by Pug, slunk onto the porch looking scared and embarrassed.

The lads told Papa about the monster that had chased them. They agreed that it was twice the size of a grizzly bear. It was fast and furry. It caught one of them by the coattail and would have killed him, but he peeled off his coat and escaped its grasp; he said its breath smelled like rotten cabbage. The next day they found its tracks. Properly primed imaginations tell fantastic fables.

Pug got swapped for a Barlow knife with one blade broken.

27

MONK EYE'S MOHAWK

My neighbor pal, Monk Eye, did everything with gusto. He possessed a wild imagination; he dreamed big dreams; he attempted impossible stunts; and his body bore trophy scars and wounds of varied shapes, sizes, age, and color.

One dog day afternoon he whizzed into my yard on his ragged old bike, slid to a stop and began jabbering so fast he was stuttering and slobbering.

He said his daddy had dropped him off in Douglasville to see a movie while he went to Austell to get some much needed 90 proof cough remedy.

A western, starring Lash LaRue and his grizzled sidekick, Fuzzy Q. Jones, was playing at the Alpha theater. LaRue was famous for his use of an 18 ft. bullwhip with which he subdued bad guys. (In later years LaRue instructed Harrison Ford in how to use the bullwhip in the Indiana Jones movies.)

In the episode Monk Eye saw, Lash LaRue and scraggly old Fuzzy Q. Jones were surrounded by savage Indians, their fearsome faces smeared with war paint. These rabid redskins had evil intentions involving giving these heroes a hatchet hair cut.

LaRue whipped his way out of trouble. The Indians fled in fear, bullwhip whelps peeking from their shredded breechcloths.

Every other boy in America would have identified with Lash LaRue, but not Monk Eye. He couldn't quit yammering about the Indians. He wanted to play cowboys and Indians, and he wanted to be an Indian in full regalia.

I made a whip from a worn out piece of plow line. A red handkerchief was my bandana, and I squished up one of Daddy's old hats for a cowboy fedora. My overalls didn't seem to compliment my outfit but Monk Eye, the cowboy expert, said at least half of them wore overalls.

He rolled up his pants legs to his thigh, and made a breechcloth out of his shirt. But he wasn't satisfied with the "look". I suggested that war paint would make him look authentic.

I "borrowed" a little tube of sample lip stick that Mama had, and put zig zags on his face, and jiggly lines down his chest. "Monk Eye, now you look jist like an Indian."

He inspected the results in Mama's handheld mirror and declared, "it still ain't right. I need my hair cut like them Indians had theirs."

I asked, "How'd they have theirs cut?"

"They had all the hair cut off to the skin except a strip right in the middle and that's whut I want. You got any scissors? I want you to give me one of them Indian hair cuts."

I got the scissors and began to whack. It was a bad looking job, even for a rookie barber. It looked like he had lost a war with a weed eater. But Monk Eye was satisfied that he looked like a genuine for real Indian.

All afternoon the woods and pasture crackled with whip and war whoops.

Mama called me to eat supper. Geronimo mounted his two wheeled pony and loped off to his teepee.

Mama Monk Eye saw him and let loose her own war whoop, misting the Indian boy with Tube Rose snuff. After getting over the shock she got tickled at the pitiful sight and couldn't bring herself to give him a whuppin'.

She scrubbed the lipstick off with turpentine, and repaired the hair cut by shaving his head.

For at least three months I could spot Monk Eye at a distance. With his whopper ears sticking out from his shiny scalp he looked like a Checker cab with both front doors open.

28

THE GHOST OF WILD BILL

I once heard an old timer tell a tale about an incident that took place in Bill Arp during the first world war. He said there was a fellow in the community, called Wild Bill, who was known to have a still; he was also known to drink up his profit. One day Wild Bill got drunk, fell off his mule and broke his neck.

Despite his weakness, he was an affable, likable man. Naturally, when he got himself dead, the community mourned. They brought food to his home, sat up night and day until the funeral, and grieved with his wife and kids.

His funeral was well attended, and the preacher remarked about all the good things about Wild Bill; he never mentioned his penchant for alcohol—no need to comment on the obvious. A sad singer sang "Precious Memories" and "Shall we gather at the river." There were few dry eyes in the church.

At the graveside the preacher recited the 23rd Psalm and the singer led the crowd in singing "Amazing Grace". Everyone went home satisfied that it had been a good funeral.

Wild Bill had a drinking buddy named Hoover. A few nights after the funeral Hoover staggered past the cemetery and saw the ghost of Wild Bill. No one believed him until a sober resident of the community was strolling by the grave yard one evening and reported seeing something like a wispy white sheet hovering over Wild Bill's grave. The rumor got traction and soon spread over the community.

There was a half witted fellow in the community, whom everyone called Snuffy. His chin bore sloppy, silent witness to his nickname.

Snuffy had two admirable qualities. He was a good hand at hog killing and he excelled at rock throwing. Some of the tall tale tellers swore they had seen him kill a rabbit on the run with a rock.

One frigid day Snuffy, along with some other men, had helped a neighbor kill a hog. The wife asked them to stay for supper. She cooked fresh tenderloin with gravy, hog brains and eggs scrambled together and hot biscuits.

A fellow named Harve didn't stay for supper. Walking home he concocted a fiendish plan. He figured he had time to go home, get a white sheet and see how fast he could make Snuffy run.

Later that night, as Snuffy approached the cemetery, the sheet clad prankster raised up making ghostly sounds. In an eerie, other worldly voice he said, "I'm the ghost of Wild Bill. I'm a'coming to git you and take you with me."

Snuffy said, "I don't care who you the ghost of, I'll knock yore head off with a rock." He picked up three or four half dollar size rocks and commenced to fling them at the ghostly apparition. One hit Harve in the forehead and stunned him. While he was getting his bearings another hit him above his eye and one hit him a glancing blow on his jaw.

He abandoned his sheet and, yelping like a panicked puppy, struck out across the cemetery doing painful damage to his shin on a tombstone.

The next day Harve hobbled to the store. He had knots on his head, a black eye, a badly skinned shin, and some sage advice for the sniggering men hanging around.

He said, "don't ever mess with a fool that ain't a'scared o' haints, and can throw a rock like a bullet. A feller could git hisself kilt."

The ghost of Wild Bill never made another appearance.

29

CRAZY CRIP AND COLD CIDER

One fall, our neighbor, Mr. Renzo Duren, and I gathered a few bushels of knotty apples and made cider, with his cider press. We divided our bounty. My portion was nearly a gallon. A Bill Arp prankster, who attempted to be a wit, and half made it, troubled me about my cider.

According to him, cider can go hard (ferment into an intoxicant). He illustrated by telling a terrible tall tale about a fellow named Crip, whom he had known during the 20s.

One year, Crip made and sold several gallons of cider. He kept a gallon for himself, which he put in the root cellar to keep cold.

One Sunday afternoon, Crip's wife, Elsie Mae, and their kids went to visit her parents. He didn't go because the sow had gotten out, and he had to catch her.

Hot and thirsty, after chasing the hog and wrestling her back into the pen, his thoughts turned to his cold cider. In the root cellar he poured a glassful, sat down on an upturned bucket, and enjoyed his cool drink. The first glass was so refreshing that he had another—and another—and another . . . .

On returning home his family heard him squalling in the root cellar. The apple elixir had sloshed over the bib of his overalls, flooded across his plug of chewing tobacco, and made a muddy track into his lap. He was jabbering, slurring his words, and attempting to sing Amazing Grace.

Elsie Mae whimpered, "He's goin' crazy, I knowed this'd happen someday, it runs on his side of family." She sent for two neighbor men, who got him in the house and onto the bed. He babbled about religion, his family, his crops, and the best cider he had ever made. One of the neighbors jumped in his T-model Ford to go to Douglasville and find a doctor. As he chugged off Elsie Mae yelled, "Tell him to hurry, Crip's a'gettin' crazier by the minute. And tell him it runs in his family."

The doctor was pried loose from a big birthday bash he was hosting for his wife. He cursed, grabbed his black bag, and crawled in the T-model. They ripped and rattled down the rutted road, that's now highway #5.

Crip prattled on, nattering about the recent war, Germans, the sorry state of the country, and how he was going to run for president, and other drivel. Elsie Mae wailed, "Crip honey, hang on, the doctor's here to hep ya get ya mind back."

The doctor rushed to the crazy man's side and began his examination. He went rigid, his face colored to a pale purple hue, a vein the size of a pencil stood taunt on his neck, and he began to swear. "What in the X*%# do you mean yanking me away from my wife's birthday party to see a #%*& blubbering drunk."

Elsie Mae said, "Oh, no doctor Crip ain't drunk; he don't drink. He's crazy. It runs in his family ya know."

"Crazy my &%#. This fool's crazy all right; he's crazy drunk." He slammed shut his bag, and stomped out, stringing expletives behind him.

A nosy neighbor proclaimed the cider to be the chaos causing culprit. Elsie Mae whined, "Crip why couldn't ya just be crazy. It runs in your family anyway." Hard cider can be hard on a marriage.

The joker's story motivated me to consume my portion of cider in a hurry, lest it get hard. Our outhouse clung to the side of a hill, about 100 feet from the house. I became skilled at the 100 foot dash. It was a moving yarn.

30

THE FLYING 'POSSUM

One of God's wonders is the flying squirrel. A fold of skin, called a patagium, stretches from the wrist of each front leg to the ankle of each rear leg. This enables the little creature to glide from tree to tree. Flights of up to 240 feet have been recorded.

Most people are aware of flying squirrels. Few, however, have ever heard of a flying 'possum. I am an exception to this ignorance; I knew one, up close and personal.

In the summer of 1953 I acquired a baby 'possum that had been abandoned by his mother. He was about the size of a mouse. I named him after Walt Kelly's comic strip character, Pogo Possum. I fixed him a cozy home in a shoe box.

Pogo became a nocturnal nuisance. He would doodle out the air hole in the box, escape and plunder the place. One morning Mama put on her apron, reached in the pocket and was horrified to shake hands with my furry friend. Another time Daddy slid his foot into a shoe occupied by a snoozing baby 'possum. Threatening clouds were thickening around Pogo and me.

The storm broke with a frenzied fury one night after we had gone to bed. Mama took exception to being awakened with a cold 'possum nose nestled against her leg. I had read *THE YEARLING* by Marjorie Kinnan Rawlings, and was beginning to identify with young Jody Baxter.

An uncle visiting from Arizona saved Pogo from the executioner. It was love at first sight when he saw the baby. He bought him from me for $2.00 and prepared to drive back home with him.

Headed west he stopped in Birmingham for a visit with his brother. He couldn't find Pogo when he got ready to leave. He searched in every 'possumy place he could think of. Time constraints compelled him to leave. He hadn't been gone but about 2 hours when Pogo crawled out from under a platform rocker.

My Birmingham uncle took care of him until his brother got home. They then made arrangements for the baby to be shipped air freight, fragile, special delivery, to Phoenix. The flying 'possum logged about 1700 miles on that flight—far outdistancing the puny 240 foot record of the flying squirrel.

My uncle and his privileged pet 'possum got along well. But one night Pogo got cold and crawled in bed with him. In his sleep he rolled over on the juvenile 'possum thus sending him to—wherever dead 'possums go.

In case the IRS reads this I need to confess that I didn't pay income tax on my 'possum pay. PETA (people for the ethical treatment of animals) hadn't yet been invented and SPCA (the society for prevention of cruelty to animals) had not yet discovered Bill Arp. But if they hear about this they may all want to stick their cold noses into the matter. Hey, I was just a kid. I didn't know about big brother.

If I have it figured right my income tax on the $2.00, plus interest and penalties compounded for 52 years comes to exactly $9,261.28. If I disappear check with the IRS, PETA or the SPCA.

31

THE SURE FIRE RED HOT CURE

    I Huddled around the pot bellied stove at Dukes store one blustery day with a couple of the regulars. One of them told a story about a fellow, named Hoss, who lived in Bill Arp during the great depression.

    Hoss was a bull of a man, John Henry, Paul Bunyan, and "Stone Cold" Steve Austin rolled into one huge hunk of manhood. Anything any other man could do he could do better, faster, and longer. He was tough. One time he made a miss lick with an ax and nearly cut his big toe off. He poured kerosene on it, wrapped it with a rag and hobbled on about his business, and never seemed to be bothered by it. The tale teller said he was swapping work with Hoss once, planting corn. He saw Hoss put a 200 pound bag of fertilizer under each arm and walk across the field with it.

    There were an abundance of stories about his larger than life exploits. One told about a big, bad billy goat that attacked him. He balled up his big old fist, that looked like a ham of meat, and smacked the goat between the eyes knocking him to his knees. When Billy awakened he clambered to his feet and got as far away from this monstrosity of a man as fast as his rubbery legs would carry him.

Much to his embarrassment, Hoss developed a bad case of hemorrhoids. Country folks called them the piles. He suffered through several bouts before his wife, Bessie, convinced him to go to the Dr. who gave him some soothing medicine to be applied for temporary relief.

One night, in pain with his perennial piles problem, he went to bed but flopped around like a dying chicken. His wife said, "Hoss why don't you jist get up and use that medicine the Dr. give to you? We need to git some sleep."

Hoss, still trying to be tough, said, "Naw, I kin handle this without that there medicine."

"I shore wish you'd do something. I'm tard and need some sleep."

The piles were stronger than Hoss. He got up. His medicine was on the mantle in the parlor. He decided not to light the kerosene lamp (electricity had not yet discovered Bill Arp). He felt his way to his bottle of soothing relief and liberally anointed his offending anatomy.

The "Watkins man" had been by that day and Hoss' wife had bought a bottle of liniment and set it on the mantle. Hoss got the wrong bottle.

He let out a war whoop and screamed, "I'm on far Bessie. Hep me." But Bessie couldn't help him—she couldn't catch him. He ran out of the house bellowing like a wounded buffalo. The trap door of his long johns flapped in the breeze like a ghost chasing him.

Bessie found him at the well sitting and soaking in the mule's watering trough. He said, "Bess when I set down in this here water hit jist fried, like bacon a'cookin', that's how hot hit was."

Later Hoss declared that this he-man treatment had forever cured him. He became evangelistic about Watkins liniment. He recommended that anybody suffering with back door problems take the liniment cure. So far no one has attempted to prove him wrong. If you choose to do so make sure you're near a mule's watering trough. And be sure to video the episode; most of us have never seen fried water.

32

THE GENUINE OFFICIAL RED RYDER BB GUN

My prized childhood possession was a genuine official Red Ryder BB gun. At Monk Eye's house I showed him my sharp shooting skill pinging a can. He was having a conniption fit to try it. I gave him all the precautions I had received. "Don't shoot that thang at nobody, you could put their eye out. Don't aim it at a dog, a cat, a hog, or nobody's mule." In spite of his history of many monumental mishaps he was always confident that he could do anything; he was certain he would be an expert shot.

He was hitting the can about once every ten shots. He said, "look how close I'm gittin'. I could hit it ever time if I wanted to." If he wanted to think he was a good shot, when the can and I knew better, let him go on in his delusion.

His daddy wasn't on friendly terms with any kind of work, so it was left up to his mama to work at the cotton mill, keep house, cook, work the garden, and put up with his whining about his many ailments, all of which required 90 proof treatment. She was a tough minded, hard working, and sometimes hard cussing, woman. She came out to work in her garden while we were plunking cans with the BB gun. She wore a pair of men's overhauls (overalls for the less cultured).

Her one joy in life was Tube Rose snuff. She would fight for it; I had seen her do it. On one occasion her husband, mad that there was no money for him to buy his medicine, (his boot legger /druggist, operated on a cash and drink basis), made a major mistake by lamenting, "we'd have money if you didn't spend it all on yore ole' snuff." She grabbed a dog wood brush broom and began whopping him and screaming expletives not intended for tender, or even not so tender, ears. It translated something like this, "you sorry low down #$%*. You wouldn't work in a %&*# pie factory. I do all the #$!*& work around heah. You spend everthang on #$@%* likker an' begrudge me my snuff." Thus ended the snuff snafu.

A small can of Tube Rose in the side pocket of her overhauls, poked out on the side of her leg as she bent over picking turnip greens. Monk Eye said, "hey, watch this, I'm 'gonna shoot mama's snuff can and scare her."

"Daggone it Monk Eye, I done tole you, don't shoot at nobody, you might put their eye out", although her eye wasn't exposed to near the hazard as other areas of her anatomy.

"Naw, I know I kin hit thet snuff can." He cocked my genuine official Red Ryder BB gun, aimed and fired. He missed the little can—he hit the big one. She yelped, jerked up board straight, and grabbed her right hip pocket.

Ever the quick thinker, in a life or death crisis, he yelled, "look out mama, Neal's done went an' stirred up a yaller jacket's nest." But she knew the source of her painful posterior problem. Kneading her abused hip pocket with one hand, she grabbed him with the other and hauled him in the house, from whence came an abundance of whopping, and an impressive string of double jointed, hide peeling cuss words. Monk Eye was bawling, like a dying calf in a hail storm. I was horrified—he still had my genuine official Red Ryder BB gun.

33

THE UNSTOLE TRUCK

Jack was an outstanding citizen of Bill Arp. He worked hard at his laborers job, came home to his family every night, was quiet and unassuming; he was a trusted and dependable neighbor; he attended church regularly where he absorbed numerous sermons warning him not to backslide.

One steamy Friday, in August, Jack had toiled for 10 hours, on his job in Atlanta, laying cement blocks. He was dehydrated and wrung out, like a dishrag. He clambered into his old 1940 Ford truck with splotched paint, floppy fenders, and a cracked windshield, and started home.

Rattling down the street Jack was lured by a flashing neon sign in a bar window. It said, "ice cold beer." He forgot about backsliding and wheeled in thinking, "I'll just drink one cold beer and go on to Bill Arp."

A few hours, and lots of cold beers, later Jack sloshed toward his truck, well hydrated—but backslidden. He maneuvered himself into the truck, got it started and zig zagged down the street.

He had puttered along almost to Austell when he made a discovery. His windshield was no longer cracked. He weaved along for another mile or two pondering this phenomenon. He looked around the cab and saw a pack of Camel cigarettes.

Jack smoked Chesterfields. A lightning bolt of understanding electrified his fuzzy brain, "this ain't my truck."

The backslidden pilferer wheeled around and headed back to the bar. With the gas gage bouncing on empty he made it back. Afraid of being caught, he parked his mistake across the street at an all night restaurant, slunk through the shadows to his real truck and tore out for Bill Arp.

On Saturday he concluded the truck was a phantom, the result of too much beer. The next week he was plagued by the "truck dream". "It kinda' seems like it was real," he thought. Jack had to have an answer. He stopped at the bar on Monday to do some detective work.

The bartender wasn't busy and began talking to him. He said, "You won't believe what happened to me Friday night. I closed up went, to go home but somebody had stole my truck." Rockets of understanding streaked through Jack's mind.

"I called the cops and while I was waiting for them I went across the street to get a cup of coffee and there sat my truck. When the cops came I explained to them that my truck had reappeared across the street from where I parked it. They talked real ugly to me and threatened to make a case against me for filing a false report." Jack took it all in nodding, shaking his head, widening his eyes, and grunting at the appropriate times.

The man said, "If that wasn't enough when I started my truck I noticed that the gas gauge was on empty. Now tell me what kind of stupid idiot would steal my truck then unsteal it after he had burned my gas?"

Jack agreed, "thieves are mighty stupid ain't they?"

He went home and made a full confession to his wife. She was so moved she wrote a poem about the episode titled *Jack's Journey*. She encouraged him to send the bartender five dollars anonymously to pay for the gas.

The preacher heard about it and came to see Jack. He said, "Jack, I'm mighty disappointed in you. What in the world made you stop at that bar anyhow?"

Shamed, Jack hung his head and said, "I don't know preacher I guess I just backfired."

34

THE SUPREME COURT OF BILL ARP

Over half a century ago Bill Arp was home to some distinguished visionaries, philosophers and profound thinkers. The Supreme Court of the United States with its pomp, pageantry and professionalism wasn't as impressive to me as were these country sages.

They reigned from Mr. Bart Dukes' store. Their seats of higher learning were empty upturned Coke and R.C. Cola cases. They smoked cigarettes rolled from Bull Durham, Prince Albert or Country Gentleman while they deliberated current concerns.

Political problems, family problems, church problems and world problems were simplified and solved around a potbellied stove. The newly won world war would have ended sooner had Roosevelt and Churchill consulted with them for their erudite solutions.

For refreshment they quaffed down Cokes with nickel bags of Planter's peanuts poured in them. The tension of laborious thinking sometimes caused one of them to take a B.C. headache powder with his Coke.

I stood in awe of these masters, with whom wisdom would die. I would nurse a Nehi orange drink and dawdle around the store for the educational stimulation. There I picked up knowledge unavailable elsewhere.

Favored subjects of the court were theology and Bible doctrine. My Nehi and I were present when one fellow, whose verbal output outperformed his mental aptitude, jutted out his chin and said, "the only part of the Bible that's true is them words printed in red."

His volatile statement brought a stir of dissent from the rest of the court. They argued this case for an hour. The Bible, the pastor, the coroner, the postman, the dry cleaning man and others of standing in the community were quoted to support their position.

One man said he knew a bootlegger who had sense enough to believe all the Bible.

The defeated dissident took two B.C. powders, left and never again had a seat around the stove. He later got a job at the thread mill in Clarkdale and moved to Cobb County. The consensus of the court was "good riddance to bad rubbish".

In another session I was educated about worming mules. I learned you should feed your mule a plug of Bloodhound chewing tobacco once a month to prevent intestinal parasites. I wondered why a tobacco eating mule wouldn't prefer Brown's mule chewing tobacco. But who was I to question a Supreme Court ruling?

In one assembly they agreed that after castrating a hog you should daub the area of the hog's loss with an aromatic elixir made of crushed red pepper, kerosene, turpentine and burnt motor oil. This was to prevent infection. You needn't worry about the hog catching an infection. There wasn't an infection around that could catch a hog anointed with this concoction. That poor porker, with blazing behind, wouldn't stop running till he ricocheted off the Alabama state line. I never heard of one thus treated getting an infection.

The years of my calendar are flipping faster than that proverbial pig's progress. The store, the stove, the sessions, and the sages are long gone. What lingers are my poignant memories of hours spent in this incomparable institution soaking up the wit, wisdom and wonder of the country store counselors.

35

MONK EYE AND THE FORTUNE TELLER

Buried in Caney Head Methodist church cemetery, in Heard county, since 1955, is a one eyed fortune teller who dubbed herself "the oracle of the ages". This never married, eccentric woman was reputed to be the wealthiest woman in Heard county. Her prowess as a fortune teller figures prominently in the best selling non fiction book *"Murder in Coweta County"* by Margaret Barnes. Her name was Mayhayley Lancaster.

Monk Eye had become intrigued with fortune tellers when his mama took him to the state fair. He got his fortune told in a side show tent. The swami told him that he would find a large sum of money beside a dirt road near a dogwood tree. He believed her.

Undeterred by the abundance of dirt roads and dogwood trees, he drew up a grid pattern of roads and began exploring them. As fate would have it, one day he found a fifty cent piece. It set him ablaze. He ripped down the road to my house on his rickety old bike yelling, "looky heah, looky heah, I done went an' fount that money that Madam Ruth tole me about."

He showed me the fifty cent piece he held in his sweaty palm. I said, "Monk Eye that ain't but fifty cents, it ain't no large sum of money."

"Hit is when you ain't got none", was his reply.

His daddy, roused by his enthusiasm, said, "I know 'bout this woman in Heard county, where I growed up. They say she's the best fortune teller in the whole world. Her name's Mayhayley Lancaster; she charges a dollar and ten cents to tell yore fortune. She says the dollar's fer her and the dime is fer her dogs."

Monk Eye said, "If I can git a dollar and a dime will you take me to Heard county? I already got fifty cents." His daddy didn't say no, he didn't say yes, but he beamed a "yes" smile at his son.

On a rainy Friday, a dollar and ten cents later, Monk Eye skipped school. Daddy Monk Eye, teetering on the edge of sobriety, had agreed to take the boy to see the famous fortune teller. After a long adventurous trip they found her house.

They were welcomed by a pack of over 30 mongrel dogs. Monk Eye waded through the pile of snarling dogs; his daddy waited in the truck. The seer met him on the ramshackle porch and took him inside.

She told him that his daddy was a drunk (Mayhayley was unyielding in her opposition to drinking) and that Monk Eye wanted him to quit more than anything. Wide eyed and head bobbing he knew that she was a prophetess.

Among other lesser important things, she told him that his daddy was going to quit drinking, get a steady job and buy him a much longed for pony. Monk Eye was ecstatic.

A week later I found a melancholy Monk Eye sitting on the back steps stroking a cat. When he saw me he said, "them fortune tellers don't know nothin'. Thet ole witch done went an' lied to me. Daddy's in yonder drunk a'gin".

He slammed the cat down, put on his 'I don't care' face and said, "I'm glad she's wrong cause I never did want no pony no how. They a lot of trouble."

Mayhayley Lancaster had a reputation as a renowned fortune teller but she misfired on that prediction and lost a convert, Monk Eye lost a pony, and his daddy lost the battle.

36

WHAT HAPPENED TO THE RUNNING BOARD?

Current cars are computer controlled cocoons. They are built for safety, get good gas mileage, and last two hundred thousand miles—but they are boring and have no personality.

I miss the cantankerous old cars, with running boards, suicide doors, curb feelers, steering knobs, manual chokes, carburetors, real bumpers, fender skirts, and continental kits. But those appendages are as rare as an ice storm in August.

The vintage vehicles didn't have turn signals. The driver rolled the window down and gave a hand signal—much different from the hand signals you get these days. The arm stuck straight out signaled a left turn, and turned up at the elbow pointing skyward indicated a right turn, and hung down meant caution.

The erratic windshield wipers were vacuum powered. When the engine was under a strain, they didn't work. They operated best on a downhill coast.

For several years our family car was a 1939 Chevrolet. It didn't have an accelerator; it had a foot feed. The parking brake was called an emergency brake. The dimmer switch was a small round silver colored, foot operated, button, on the floor, to the left of the clutch. The starter was engaged by pressing a foot peg on the right side of the brake pedal. It didn't need a computer; it had a mind of its own.

For short trips daddy sometimes hauled 14 people in that old sedan. Eight would squeeze inside. Two would stand on each running board, and one would sit on each front fender, straddling a headlight. The government had not yet discovered danger, so we were unencumbered with safety devices and regulations.

One Sunday we were coming home from church with a light load of passengers. We had our family of five, a neighbor family of three, and one teenage boy, who was spending the afternoon with my brother, Ronald. He and his friend volunteered to ride the running boards.

A slow Saturday rain had turned Big A road into a loblolly of mud. We were squishing along, almost home, when a blue tick hound bounded in front of us. Daddy braked hard and turned the steering wheel to avoid the dog. The car lurched sideways and slid to a sloppy stop. My brother's buddy, whom I'll call Edward, was catapulted off the running board like a cannon ball. He arched through the air and made a splatty, rolling landing.

Like a mud monster, he slithered out of the slop, making wild gestures and squealing unintelligible words, sentences, paragraphs, and whole essays. His anger was directed at the running board. He shook his fists at it, slinging mud in all directions. He bent down face to face with it. He jabbed his finger at it. He fussed at it. He fumed over it. He scolded it. He rebuked it. There's never been a running board to get such a chastening.

He sputtered to the end of his undecipherable oratory and said, "Mr. Beard, you oughta git that old running board fixed afore somebody gits hurt. That thang's done went and throwed me like a wild hoss."

Edward, the muddy mess, mounted a front fender. The blue tick faded into a cornfield. The running board offered no defense against the charge.

37

THE TWICE STOLE SHOTGUN SHELLS

In the spring of 1837 Nathaniel Hawthorne published *Twice Told Tales*, a short story collection in two volumes. They were from previously published periodicals. Unlike Hawthorne's tales mine is pristine; it has never been published; it has rarely been told. It's a true account of twice stole shells.

There used to be a fellow in Bill Arp who had a reputation for having "sticky fingers". I'll use the fictitious name of Floyd in referring to him. He would steal when the right opportunity presented itself.

Floyd bought his gas, groceries, and necessities, such as B.C. headache powders, at Mr. Bart Dukes store. He sometimes took his meals at the store. He would dine on sardines, potted meat, or Vienna sausages and soda crackers. An R.C. Cola "belly washer" was his drink of choice.

One day a friend of mine, whom I'll call Jack, was in the back of the store and saw Floyd come in. He sauntered over to the counter where the sardines, potted meat, and Vienna sausages were shelved. Across the aisle, against the wall was a shelf where Mr. Bart stocked shot gun shells and 22 rifle bullets. Floyd looked around, thought no one was looking, and slid a box of 16 gauge shot gun shells under his floppy denim jacket. He paid for his snack and left with the shells still nestled under his coat.

This theft occurred at a time when there had been a death in the community. In those days it was customary for the undertaker to prepare the body and return it home. Friends and family would sit up around the clock until the funeral. Ladies would bring loads of food and the wake would usually turn into a time of eating, fellowship, and tale telling.

Some of the folks seemed glad, in a sad way, when there was a death. It was like an all day singing with "dinner on the grounds". People got a chance to eat the best vittles prepared by the best cooks in the community. Though it never seemed respectful to me, they had a good time at these "settin' ups", as most folks called them. Funny stories, jokes, yarns of all descriptions, and teasing were common fare at these events. Floyd never missed a "settin' up". Floyd lived alone so the "settin' up" food was a monumental improvement over his own fare, and it afforded him an opportunity to socialize.

One night during the wake Jack went to take a turn "settin' up". Among the eight or ten vehicles there he spotted Floyd's rusty old truck. He decided to search the truck to see if the stolen shotgun shells might be in it. He slid his hand under the seat on the driver's side and felt the box of shells. He put them in his car and went in the house.

The next day Jack went to Mr. Bart's store with the box of shells secreted under his coat. He strolled around to the shell shelf and placed them back in their place. The shells were stolen, re-stolen, returned and Mr. Bart never knew they had been on vacation.

A man who worked with Floyd later told about him coming to work one morning later in the week and complaining about someone stealing a box of shotgun shells right out of his truck. He said Floyd gave the thief a real good cussin' and went on for a while about how bad the world's getting.

38

MONK EYE AND THE STAR OF BETHLEHEM

Monk Eye, in spite of a string of mishaps, considered himself an expert on animal husbandry. He planned to get a job at the cotton mill and save enough money to go to veterinarian school. He said, "much as I already know I won't have to go to school long".

A coonhound suffering from a severe case of mange wandered into Monk Eye's yard one day. Finally, a case worthy of his skills. He called him Itchy. I rode up on my bike while he was assessing his patient. I said, "Monk Eye whatcha' 'gonna do with thet mangy ole' dog."

"I know whut to do. You jist watch me."

He tied the dog to a tree and went in the house and got a wash pan. He crawled under the house and came out with a gallon jug of something that looked like blackstrap molasses. "Whut's thet stuff Monk Eye?"

"This heah's burnt motor oil. I'm a'gonna mix some sulphur with it and daub it on Itchy and hit'll cure him of the mange." His mama kept a sack of sulphur to keep insects off her apple tree. He got it and poured about a cup full in the wash pan. He mixed in about a quart of burnt motor and began sopping it on Itchy.

When the job was done Monk Eye attempted to wash the pan. But the oil wouldn't wash off. "Mama's a'gonna whup me when she gits home if I don't git this heah wash pan clean."

I said, "maybe you can git a rag and wipe it out real good an' clean an' she won't know nuthin' about it."

"Yeah, yeah, thet's whut I'll do. Now I gotta' find me a rag."

He went in the house and came back with a patched up looking piece of material. "This is jist a bunch uv scrap pieces uv cloth thet mama's sewed together." He wiped the wash pan out and put it back in the kitchen.

He dropped the rag beside the back steps, and was admiring his handiwork on Itchy when his mama and daddy rattled up in their old truck. She looked at Itchy, spat a stream of Tube Rose ambeer, and said, "Monk Eye, whut in the world have you done to thet dog?"

"I doctored him mama. An' soon's he gits his hair growed back out I'm a'gonna sell him for $25."

She started up the back steps shaking her head, and saw the rag. She picked it up and screeched a stream of obsenities not meant for timid souls or tender ears. "You've rurnt my Star of Bethlehem quilt top. I'm a'gonna skin you alive boy. Yore granny made thet quilt top fer me."

I felt compelled to scamper on home. I straddled my bike and left Monk Eye to face death alone. I could hear him caterwauling like a lonesome tom cat, as I pedaled toward my safe haven.

The next day he told me she whipped him till his daddy made her stop. Then she went in the house and discovered the greasy wash pan and would have beat him some more, but in her rage she had swallowed some Tube Rose and had to lie down for a while.

The dog got well; Monk Eye sold him for $20; and all it cost was a near death experience and a Star of Bethlehem quilt top.

He reported to me, "Didn't I tell you I could git thet dog well?"

39

MONK EYE'S MARBLE MEAL

On those rare occasions when Monk Eye elected to attend school he brought his lunch in a brown paper bag. The lunch fixings his mama bought were peanut butter, bananas, mayonnaise, and crushed pineapple. She favored the pineapple.

Other kids would swap goodies from their lunches but most people weren't interested in a soggy pineapple sandwich so Monk Eye rarely got to do any lunch exchanges.

Bill Arp school didn't have playground equipment so we kids devised our own games. Girls played jump rope and jackstones a lot. Boys wrestled, played chase, and shot marbles.

There was a school rule against playing marbles for keeps. It was considered gambling. And most of our parents had forbidden it; so, we played for keeps. In doing so each shooter keeps all the marbles he knocks out of the ring. Obviously the best shot wins the most marbles.

Monk Eye had more self confidence than gumption, and he had an array of scars to prove it. He couldn't accept that he wasn't the best at whatever he attempted. He assumed he was good at marbles, and challenged the school champ, a pudgy boy nicknamed Joy.

Monk Eye had about 40 marbles in his pocket. Each boy put five in the center of the ring. In the first round he won four marbles. The champ's strategy was to hold back till Monk Eye's confidence was over inflated then clean him out.

In the second round Monk Eye won three more marbles. His head was getting big. I said, "Monk Eye, I done seen Joy play marbles before and he's settin' you up to win all yore marbles."

Monk Eye was inspired. He said, "Shud up. You're jist jealous cause you can't play marvels good as me."

"Daggone it, Monk Eye, I'm tryin' to hep ya keep from losin'. Joy's agonna take everthang you got if you don't quit while you're ahead."

Monk Eye had fire in his eyes. He was bouncing around, like a monkey on a rubber rope. He bragged to the boys who had gathered to watch the game, "old Joy's agonna go home with his pockets empty today. He jist ain't never played nobody good as me."

Monk Eye only salvaged one marble in the next game and then never got another. Soon the empty pockets were his. Like most gamblers he thought his luck would change next time.

He said, "Les play jist one more game."

Joy said, "How you gonna play without marbles?"

Monk Eye said, "You put 20 marvels in the ring and we'll shoot. If I get the most I get to keep all 20. If you get the most you can have my lunch." Joy usually ate his lunch at recess and then bummed food off other kids at lunchtime. His stomach growled favorably at this prospect.

Monk Eye fidgeted and mumbled as Joy knocked the last marble out of the ring. He handed over his lunch and slouched off grumbling, "I'm jist like my daddy I ain't never had no luck cept for bad luck."

At lunch time I was eating a peanut butter and banana sandwich. Monk Eye looked so pitiful I tore it in half and shared it with him. "Monk Eye, now you done went and lost ya marbles and ya lunch. What kind of sandwich did you have anyway?"

He said, "Mama didn't have no pineapples so she made me a collard sandwich."

A queasy Joy sat on the other side of the lunchroom pondering the sad consequences of gambling.

40

THE PARTY LINE

    I remember a pure, pristine and peaceful time when people didn't carry their phone in purse or pocket. None of our leading luminaries envisioned a day when you would carry a phone on your person. Had you suggested it you would have been a candidate for a white sport coat with wrap around sleeves. Your lodging would have been a rubber room.

    It seems we didn't need to talk as much then as we do now. Until the late '40's and early '50's our communication choices in Bill Arp were limited. You talked to folks at church, the store or sent a penny post card. For more serious communication a letter, requiring a three cent stamp, was sent.

    That all changed when Ma Bell came bellowing into the community draping her rubber coated wire over the shoulders of the utility poles. She made it possible for us to talk to Douglasville, Fairplay, Winston, Lithia Springs and every other niche of the county. To call outside the county was long distance.

    The clunker phones were heavy enough for boat anchors. They were owned by Southern Bell. Color choices were black, black or black. Our first service was an eight party line. That's eight families using one line. It's like having one line with eight extensions.

Each party had a different ring to distinguish their calls from the other seven. Our ring was one long and one short. It was common practice for everyone on the party line to listen in when anyone else got a call. There was proper protocol to be observed when listening in on someone else's call. You never picked up the receiver till the ringing stopped, indicating they had answered. You didn't just jerk it up either. You gently lifted the receiver. You didn't breathe into the phone or make any noise. All knew everybody else was listening but etiquette dictated that everybody pretend nobody was listening.

One person on our party line—I'm using a fictitious name to protect the guilty—was Charlie. On rare occasions Charlie was guilty of being sober. When Charlie was drunk he didn't use proper "listening in" decorum. Charlie would get on the line when Mama was using it. He would pick up and start dialing. Mama knew who it was. "Charlie, I'm using the phone now. Hang up please. You can have the line in a few minutes."

"Ish that you Mrs. Beard?" he would slur.

"Yes it's me now get off the line please."

"How's Mr. Beard doin' these days?"

"He's fine. Now get off the line and let me talk."

"I ain't seen him since Buck was a calf. He still work at P.F. Goodrish?"

"Charlie, you know he works at B.F. Goodrich. Now please get off the line."

"How them boys doin'?"

On and on it would go. The person mama was talking to had to wait while she coaxed Charlie to quit interrupting. When Mama's wheedling didn't work she would detonate her lethal weapon. She would blast him off the line with the Bible. When he was drunk the Bible made him cry. She would begin quoting it to him—it didn't matter which book, chapter or verse. "Charlie did you know the Bible says . . . ." He would blubber, "I gotta' go Mrs. Beard" and hang up.

The Good Book has kept many from taking up drink. It's strengthened others to over come the addiction. But Charlie's the only one I ever knew who got off the party line because of the Bible.

41

THE BLUE TAILED YELLOW JACKET

My maternal grandfather, Papa Jones, lived with us off and on for years. He and we boys attempted farming while daddy worked a public job.

In 1947 daddy bought us a big red horse named Bill. He was a beautiful animal and a good plow horse, but he was skittish; anything out of the ordinary would spook him and he would run away.

One scalding, hot day, Papa was "laying by" a field of corn (for the inadequately educated, and the Philistines, amongst us the final plowing of a crop was called "laying it by"). I was too young to help with the fieldwork; my assignment was to carry Papa a quart of cool well water in mid-morning and in mid-afternoon.

In Papa's memory bank was an occasion when he had plowed up a yellow jacket's nest and paid for it many times over. He was hurriedly unhitching his mule from the plow to escape when the nasty tempered little monsters discovered the mule and started popping him. He thought Papa was hurting him and kicked him on the shin. Ever after Papa was vexed with a fear of the demonic like pests.

On this sweltering afternoon I was delivering Papa's water. In those days I had a sharp eye for wild life. I spotted a little black snake stalking a blue tailed lizard. (I've now learned that they are called blue tailed skinks.) I never cared for the predator/prey aspect of wild life; a well chunked rock chased the snake away.

The lizard, glad to have missed lunch with the predator, was frantically vacating the scene of his near demise. Papa had stopped Bill next to where I was standing. His pants leg blossoming out over his old shoes looked like a safe haven to the lizard. The blue tail scampered into this dark retreat.

Papa, feeling the lizard wriggling up his leg, thought he had gotten into yellow jackets. He went wild, whooping, hollering, dancing about, and beating his pants. This further excited the lizard who made several circuits inside his trousers. Papa, stomping, yelling, and slapping, shucked off his britches.

He still had the plow lines looped around his wrists. The commotion scared Bill. He lunged forward jerking papa down on his face. The terrorized horse ran for the barn, dragging the plow stock and papa. I did the only thing I knew to do—nothing.

About twenty feet later Papa was able to shake loose from the plow lines. He was stretched out on his stomach; his britches were bunched up around his ankles. His sweat and the dirt made him look like a chocolate covered streaker. Bill was nearing the barn. Papa was nearing tears.

I drew up in a knot. An event, such as I had witnessed, would normally put Papa in a cussing mode; when properly provoked he could cuss the bark off a pine tree. But he didn't utter one swear word. Apparently some good can come from a case of terminal humiliation.

Realizing he hadn't been stung he started getting himself back together. As he was shaking the dirt out of his pants a dead lizard fell out. The little fellow had been squashed in the turmoil. He might as well have lunched with the snake.

Had I let nature take its course Papa wouldn't be standing there looking like a mud ball, Bill wouldn't be trembling in the barn, and the snake would have had lunch.

I said, "Papa, I brought you a drink of water." He wasn't thirsty.

42

MONK EYE'S GIANT RABBIT BOX

We used to catch rabbits in homemade traps we simply called rabbit boxes. One blustery day, probably about 1951, I was building a rabbit box. Monk Eye rattled up on his junky old bicycle and said, "What'cha doin'?"

"I'm buildin' me a new rabbit box cause an ole possum rurnt mine. I ain't usin' nothin' but hard corn for bait from now on cause them ole possums will eat cabbage, lettuce and apple cores, but they won't eat hard corn, 'an I don't wanna catch no more possums."

In typical Monk eye fashion, he got excessively exuberant about building himself a rabbit box. I checked on his progress the next day. He was building it out of twelve inch wide boards. I said, "Monk Eye them boards is too wide. You tryin' to ketch a hog?"

He said, "If you wanna catch a big rabbit you gotta have room for him to git in the box."

"Monk Eye, that jist ain't no way to build a rabbit box."

"You ever caught a giant rabbit?"

"Naw, cause they ain't no sich thang as a giant rabbit."

"I'll show you when I ketch me one."

He baited his box with hard corn, cabbage, lettuce, and an apple core.

One day I went with him to check his rabbit box. The trigger had been thrown; the door had slammed shut; Monk Eye was ecstatic.

I said, "You probly' caught ya'self a possum in thet thang."

"I ain't caught no possum. I caught me a big ole' fat rabbit."

He whizzed to the box, tilted it back, yanked up the door and peered in at his prize. It wasn't a rabbit; it wasn't a possum; it was an outraged skunk. Insulted by the disrespect shown him he greeted Monk Eye with an odoriferous spray. My scrappy little dog Jip got one whiff, yelped and headed for home like his tail was afire. I hadn't been close enough to get sprayed but I was close enough to know that I didn't want to get close enough.

Monk Eye rolled on the ground hollering, "hep me."

"I can't hep you."

He heaved; he groaned; he whimpered; he stank. The offended little animal marched out of the box and with head held high, trotted off, stopping to look back and sneer at Monk Eye.

Those deluded by evolution say the skunk developed over 40 or 50 million years. These expert skunkologists say that before a skunk sprays it will go through a series of threat maneuvers including stamping their front feet. This particular skunk hadn't evolved to the point of a foot stamping warning; but it had built up 50 million years worth of concentrated stink, which he freely shared with Monk Eye

He heaved and gagged all the way home. I followed at a safe upwind distance. His mama made him go to the woods and strip off naked. She filled a wash tub in the yard, and threw him a wash cloth and a bar of lye soap; and kept a safe distance from her aromatic son, while he scrubbed and squalled.

She doused him in tomato juice to unstink him; it didn't. Time finally proved effective in fumigating the odorous boy.

Several aroma free days later I asked, "Monk Eye, what'cha gonna do with that big ole rabbit box?"

He said, "Mama said I can't ketch nothing else. You ken have it."

Somewhere in a honeysuckle patch off Big A road I own a gigantic rabbit box—that's had limited use.

43

LESSON LEARNED IN A WATERMELON PATCH

Heavy, hearty, and heavenly—that's how I remember Mr. Renzo Duren's watermelons in the '40's and '50's. They had thin rinds and sweet meat. The fanciest French cuisine was three day old collards compared to these gourmet delicacies.

The Durens were our closest neighbors. Mr. Renzo, Mrs. Ora and their daughter, Verdine, lived on a farm at the corner of Big A road and Kings Highway. Mr. Duren plowed his fields with a crotchety horse named Bob.

My neighborly duties each year included helping him save seeds from his best melons. Verdine would call, "daddy says he needs a boy to help him with a little job." That meant he was going to cut one of those behemoths. He would get the melon out from under the bed in their spare bed room, where it had been kept for a couple of days to cool off. Mrs. Ora would give me a pie pan to put my seeds in. They were black as crow's heads.

The fragrance from the massive melons activated my saliva glands like artesian wells. Luscious nectar dripped off my chin and arms. The flavor is etched in the memory of my taste buds. There's never been a boy who helped his neighbor with more gusto than I. Mr. Renzo always complimented me on a job well done.

One full moon evening a fellow conspirator and I decided it would be fun to raid Mr. Renzo's watermelon patch—*steal from the good man who would give me all the melons I wanted* (that's brilliant). Under the light of the big moon we each selected a large melon. We lugged them into the edge of the woods, cut them and began eating the warm, sweet flesh.

It was the best of melons, it was the worst of melons (forgive me Charles Dickens). It was a good melon—but not to me. Mrs. Fannie Spinks, my Sunday school teacher at Prays Mill Baptist church, had been teaching us the ten commandments. She lingered long on the eighth, "Thou shalt not steal." That Biblical admonition was reverberating in my head. Every bite was a sermon to my soul. An eternity later, assaulted by a glut of guilt, I finished that melon of misery.

My burdensome boil of backsliding came to a head the next day. Mr. Renzo and I had robbed a bee tree. After we got out of range of the irate bees we sat down on a log to rest and eat some of our bounty. I snaked my hand into my pocket for my knife to cut a piece of honeycomb. Puzzled, I said, "my knife's gone." Mr. Renzo said, "I've got it," and handed me my pearl handled Barlow. *"I found it this morning in my watermelon patch."*

Horror hurtled through my heart, squeezed my throat and set my face afire. I was saturated with shame. I attempted to sputter an apology but he waved it off. He winked at me, patted me on the back with a sticky hand and said, "You have to be careful where you lose your knife." He seemed to forget my indiscretion. I never have.

44

MONK EYE, MUMBLETY PEG, AND MUD

The government has decreed that a boy who brings a pocketknife to school is a wanted, wild west desperado, a bank robber, a serial killer, a terrorist, a putrid influence on society, and a danger to old ladies, all rolled into one malcontented, maniacal, mischief maker. The guilty are expelled from school and exiled to outer Slobovia until the next 500 year flood.

Before "big brother" most boys carried a pocketknife. At Bill Arp school we swapped knives, threw knives, and played mumblety peg.

This is a game where the player flips the knife from a number of prescribed positions, the object being to stick the blade in the ground. If the player fails on any move, he loses his turn and the other boy plays. The winner is the first to make it through every position.

The victor hits a wooden peg three times with the back of his knife, driving it as deeply into the ground as possible. The loser has to dig it out with his teeth. Gritty, red dirt smiles identify losers.

Monk Eye bragged that he was the best mumblety peg player in all of Bill Arp; and he was good. With his long thin bladed knife he had never lost.

A wiry, red headed, pug nosed, strip of a boy, named Donny, enrolled at Bill Arp in 1950; he was tough as a pine knot. A bully threatened him on his first day and got a bloody nose and a fat lip as souvenirs.

No one, except Monk Eye, ever confronted the boy again; he dared him to play mumblety peg. The red headed boy had a pitiful looking old Barlow knife. The blade was wobbly, and brass brads stubbed up where fake pearl handles had once resided.

It was a rainy day and the schoolyard was sloppy with red mud. Monk Eye grinned and said to me, "Did you see that ole knife Red's got? I hope he likes eatin' mud."

Monk Eye played first. With a bold smirk he said, "I'm a'goin' all the way Red." He held the knife in the palm of his up turned hand; with a skillful flip it stuck in the ground. He expertly executed one position after another until he got to his chin. In this position he held his thumb against his chin, placed the knifepoint on the ball of his thumb and flipped the knife. It stuck in the mud at an angle, slowly tilted and fell.

Red started through the moves, and it was evident why his old Barlow was worn out. This wasn't his first time to play mumblety peg. The last play was to drop the knife over the shoulder. Like a guided missile, with a red mud fetish, the Barlow found its mark. Monk Eye looked queasy.

The rickety knife drove the peg out of sight. Grumbling and grousing Monk Eye began biting and spitting red mud until he pulled the peg out. His face was awash with mud. It was in his eyebrows, up his nose, and in his teeth. Any sow would have been proud to claim him.

Monk Eye wasn't prone to admit defeat. As he passed through the crowd of snickering boys he said, "he wouldn't of won if he didn't have that big 'ole heavy knife."

The Bible says, *"Pride goeth before destruction and an haughty spirit before a fall"*. The contemporary interpretation is, "don't challenge a fellow with a worn out knife—unless you have a taste for red mud.

45

SAVING MONKEYE

One of the few pleasures in the harsh life of Monk Eye's mama was dipping snuff. One day she told Monk Eye to ride his bicycle to the store, in Bill Arp, and get her a can of Tube Rose. She was out.

Mama Monk Eye went to the cupboard, where she stashed her mad money in a pint jar; she began swearing. Her husband had "borrowed" it to get some of his 90 proof medicine. He received a champion cussin' in abstentia.

She had fifty cents in her pocket book that she planned to mete out during the week buying Cokes to go with her lunch. She said, "I can get by without Cokes but I can't get by without snuff." She gave Monk Eye the fifty cents to get her snuff.

I rode to the store with him; I had a dime that wanted to be spent. I could get a Baby Ruth candy bar for a nickel and a Nehi orange drink with the other nickel.

I didn't give a thought to sharing with Monk Eye. He dawdled around eyeing the candy and watching me hog down my goodies. He struggled with a swirling whirlpool of temptation; he gave up and was dragged under.

He said, "I'm gittin' me some candy."

I said, "Monk Eye, you can't do that yore mama'll kill ya'."

"I don't care. She don't need no old snuff no how. She don't never buy me no candy so I'm spendin' this here money on me."

He ate two Eskimo pie ice cream bars, a moon pie, a Zagnut candy bar, and a Butter Finger. He chased it with a Pepsi Cola, and took his change in bubble gum.

The doomed boy and I rode toward judgment. As we got close to home he started blubbering. He said, "I done went and messed up bad. Mama's gonna' kill me fer shore. She gits real mean when she ain't got no snuff, and she's already mad cause daddy done went and stole her money"

I said, "maybe you can give her a piece of bubble gum."

He was cotton white when we got to his house.

He said, "Go in with me. Mama might not whup me too bad if you're with me."

Halfway up the back steps his stomach rebelled against the ice cream, the candy, the Pepsi, and the nerves. He draped over the handrail and blasted out a volcanic eruption that may have included his toenails.

His mama hurtled down the steps. "Whut's the matter with Monk Eye?"

I blustered, "I don't know what's the matter with him. We was going to the store and he was holdin' the fifty cents real tight in his fist cause he didn't want to lose it, and all of a sudden he turned white and started weaving, then his bicycle run in the ditch. I think he passed out. But when I pulled him out of the ditch he had lost the fifty cents. We looked and looked but we never did find it. Monk Eye was so sick I brought him back home.

She helped him up the steps. "Honey don't you worry about no fifty cents I jist want my baby to be all rite." Monk Eye gazed at me like I was the governor who had issued a last minute pardon as the electric chair loomed in the background. His pasty face began to show signs of survival.

A theologian couldn't untangle my conflicted emotions. Is it okay to lie to save a life?

46

THAT WAS NO LADY, THAT WAS MY HORSE

Being rural raised in the 40s and 50s had distinct advantages. I don't remember what they were; but when I complained about the farm work, daddy reminded me of their character building qualities. Of course he didn't farm; he worked in Atlanta and left the farming to my granddaddy, my brother, and me.

Daddy thought if a boy plowed a mule all day, he wouldn't get into devilment at night. He was right. Our mule, Jack, never went carousing at night. He never used tobacco or alcohol; nor did he swear.

A mule is a hybrid animal. He's half jackass and half horse—not unlike some people you may know, be related to, or voted for.

Donkeys have 62 chromosomes; horses have 64. When bred together the offspring have 63, a number that can't be divided equally, therefore mules are sterile.

Mules have the sure footedness, patience and endurance of a donkey, and the vigor and strength of a horse. They can be maintained on less food than a horse. These characteristics make them preferable to horses for work animals.

Mules respond to a different language than other people. When you're plowing a mule you don't give it directions by saying, "go right mule", or "go left mule". Gee is mule talk to step to the right. Haw, he understands, means step to the left.

Daddy—the one who didn't farm—sold Jack, the gentleman mule, and bought a horse. She was a big, fast walking, high strung, gray horse named Lady—but she wasn't. She was strong enough to pull up Stone mountain by the roots.

My granddaddy, or my brother, could plow her all day without a problem, but not me.

When I was plowing she had little respect for gee and haw. If I said gee she might gee, she might haw, she might go straight, or she might stop.

One scalding, hot day I was "laying by" a field of corn. Most crops got two or more plowings during growing season. The last plowing was called "laying by" the crop. Revivals at church were timed to begin after "laying by" time, when farmers had a break before harvest.

Lady had been cantankerous all morning. I was tired of her smashing the corn with her big feet; she was tired of me shrieking gee, and haw. After one of my verbal assaults, she stopped, refused to budge, turned her head and gave me a defiant glare that said . . . I won't say what it said; I don't use that kind of language.

Pushed over the edge, as any normal person would have been, I grabbed a fist sized rock and blasted her rear end with it. Coincidentally, she chose that exact moment to run away. She headed for the barn at a lope dragging the plow and tearing down corn. I steamed for home—and the shotgun.

Mama was waiting with Lady when I fumed into the barnyard. Her demeanor told me to forget the shotgun; she had taken sides with the horse in our harmless little feud. She ripped a limb off a pear tree and, as she said, taught me to control my terrible temper tantrums.

Had Lady had one less chromosome my disposition and dignity would have been salvaged. She would have been a mule—and a lady.

47

A DAY THAT WILL LIVE IN INFAMY

Our history is peppered with unforgettable days. On April 4, 1861 the shot was fired that launched the civil war. December 7, 1941 the Empire of Japan bombed us into World War II. November 11, 1963 President Kennedy was assassinated. Not forgotten are the terrorist attacks of September 11, 2001. My personal "day of infamy" is June 6, 1958. That day I, an innocent 17 year old, enlisted in the United States Air Force.

Master sergeant Mitchell came to Douglas County High, with an Air Force recruitment appeal. I left that day with a fist full of Air Force literature, and an appointment with sergeant Mitchell in his temporary Douglasville office. He welcomed me with a firm handshake, a snaky smile, and addressed me as Mr. Beard. He asked, "Where would you like to be stationed if you join with us?"

I said, "I'd like to be stationed close to home." He guaranteed my permanent assignment would be Dobbins, Moody, Hunter, or Warner Robbins, all bases in Georgia.

He said, "Mr. Beard, do you have any career preference?" I thought a career in electronics would be nice. He said, "You got it."

After graduation I went to the military processing center in Atlanta for two days of testing. A lieutenant dismissed me and said, "Mr. Beard come back on June 6, at 9:00 A.M. to be sworn in.

That morning I raised my right hand and took an oath administered by a captain. I lowered my hand and he said, "here's a ticket for a 2:30 P.M. flight to San Antonio. If you miss that flight you will be AWOL. You will be arrested by the military police, serve up to three years in prison at hard labor, and given a dishonorable discharge." He didn't call me Mr. Beard.

I, along with about a dozen others, was met in San Antonio by staff sergeant Colley (he should have been named sergeant pit bull). He was angry because he had to be at the airport at 1:00 A.M. He lined us up and cussed for a while. He informed us that he would be our training instructor (TI) for the next 11 weeks. He said, "I'll be your mama and your daddy." Until then I had always loved them.

We were taken to the base and assigned bunks. Sleep came around 3:00 A.M. Two garbage can lid cymbals awakened us at 5:00 A.M. Weeks of similar sad circumstances followed.

The promised electronics school became hydraulics maintenance school. The Georgia base was a flight line assignment at Sonderstrom Air Force base on the artic island of Greenland.

If still living, Sergeant Mitchell would be in his 90s now. A lesser man than I might dream of meeting him one day and asking, "Do you remember me? You promised me electronics training and an assignment in Georgia. Instead I was a hydraulics mechanic in the artic."

This lesser man would enjoy seeing horror creep across the old sergeant's wrinkled features as he recognizes a 17 year old country boy whom he deceived; a tear drips off his quivering chin. He says, "please forgive me. All these years my scalding conscience has plagued me."

I would never entertain the thought of pushing an old sergeant down a flight of stairs into a shark filled pool of ice water because of something that happened 49 years, 6 months, 28 days, 6 hours, and 4 minutes ago. I'm not one to hold grudges. One must forgive and forget. I'm Mr. Beard.

48

A BULLDOG NAMED COLLEY

The climactic battle of World War II began on June 6, 1944—the day on which the invasion of Normandy, on the northern coast of France, began. It started the successful Western Allied effort to liberate mainland Europe from Nazi occupation. That historic, day when history's hinge could have bent in either direction, was dubbed D-Day.

Exactly 14 years later on June 6, 1958 my personal D-Day occurred. I was liberated from the mundane life of milking a cow, feeding hogs, and being subservient to my parents. With the ink barely dry on my Douglas County High diploma, I raised my right hand and was inducted into the U.S. Air Force. I had achieved adulthood; I was free at last.

During the three week recruitment process I was always called Mr. Beard. I lowered my hand and was never again referred to as Mr. Beard. The captain said, "you have a plane to catch at 2:30 P.M. If you miss it you will be AWOL." I didn't know what that was, but his scowl made me think I didn't want to be guilty of it.

I arrived in San Antonio in the small hours of the day. A dozen or so other liberated recruits, from different parts of the country, were arriving as well. We were pointed to an Air

Force bus in the parking lot where we met bleary-eyed Staff Sgt. Colley, who would be our T.I. (training instructor).

Sgt. Colley lined us up beside the bus and broke bad on us. We were recipients of some serious cussing. He cussed about having to get out of bed and come to the airport at 1:00 A.M. to pick up a load of soft sissies, who would most likely receive dishonorable discharges. He cussed us for all the trouble we would be to him for the next 11 weeks. He cussed us because, he predicted, most of us would never learn to march properly. He used double barreled, newly minted, loose jointed, cuss words with curly cues on the end, to describe what would happen if anyone even thought of going AWOL (that AWOL is a bad thing).

He fumed and cussed for half an hour, telling us how for the next 11 weeks he would be our only family. A storm cloud hung black and threatening over my liberation.

We pillowed our heads around 3:00 A.M., with our ears ringing from Sgt. Colley's verbal obscenities. He awakened us at 5:00 A.M. by clanging two garbage can lids together next to our heads while emptying his cuss word cache on us.

The Sgt. then herded us to the mess hall (appropriately named). We side stepped down the chow line as K.P.'s slammed slop onto our trembling trays. With little sleep, bug eyed with fright, and a knotted stomach I didn't feel like eating. Sgt. Collie saw me about to dump my food, and, from some deep well of reserve, he hauled up a bucketful of virgin cuss words, and painted a gloomy picture of what would happen to me if I ever took food that I didn't eat.

And so it went for 11 endless weeks. Too late I discovered that D-Day stood for disaster, defeat, discouragement, doom, and perhaps death.

We're indebted to General Eisenhower's troops on their success that began on June 6, 1944. However, on D-Day 1958 history's hinge, greased with liberal gobs of cuss words, swung in another direction, without a squeak, and left me wondering, "what kind of mother would name her bulldog, Colley?"

49

BIG BERTHA THE BITTER BARBER

For years my head has been an experimental lab for an array of barbers. I have survived weed eater specialists, atom bomb, mushroom cloud stylists; and homemade haircuts, with hand squeezed clippers. But the most harrowing hair cut I ever survived was flung on me by a rabid female barber.

Barbers, by the way, are more qualified for congress than the current crop making mischief with our money. Before he can cut hair the barber has to go to school to learn his craft and be licensed by the state. Politicians don't have to go to school; they don't even have to be licensed. My dog has to have a license.

I like most barbers, but I would prefer to be scalded and plucked like a chicken before I let one barber cut my hair again.

My old barber had gone out of business. Seeking a new one I sauntered into an unfamiliar shop. I was surprised that no customers were there on a late Friday afternoon. No barber was in sight either. I turned to leave when a semi-feminine voice thundered from a back room, "I'll be there in a minute."

I picked up a 9 year old *Field & Stream* magazine but before I could sit down the barrel shaped barberette blustered in. She had frizzy red hair that had been styled with an eggbeater, a red checkered shirt, bib overalls, and a pair of yellow brogans. She had been eating or drinking something and had foam around her mouth. She looked like a rabid logger.

Indicating the middle chair she roared "sit down right there." I sat—but soon wished I had run. She cinched the cloth around my neck tighter than the middle band on a bale of cotton. Clouds of whiskey soaked breath drifted around my head.

She bellowed, "Is that too tight?"

I wheezed, "a little."

She jammed a sausage shaped finger between my neck and the cloth and said, "naw, that ain't too tight."

She clamped a meaty hand on my head and started cutting and cussing. She hated men. Men were, according to her, the sorriest, slimiest, good for nothing creatures that God ever made. She wasn't mad that her husband had gone grizzly bear hunting in Canada, or that he had taken the trailer payment, the truck payment, his last pay check, and filled up their credit cards to fund the trip. She was livid that he slipped off without her. "Ain't that just like a no good piece of trash of a man? I been married three times and I know men. They're sorry as gully dirt.", she slurred. I was praying she wouldn't notice that I was of the male persuasion.

She began stropping a straight razor to shave around my ears. My heart was beating like a jack hammer. Beads of sweat the size of pinto beans popped out on my face.

She now transposed from cussing mad to crying mad. "Why wouldn't he take me?", she sobbed, throwing her arms wide in a dramatic gesture, whizzing the razor past my captive ear.

What would I look like with an ear missing? If she lopped of both of them my hat would fall down over my eyes and I would be blind.

Finally finished, she tore the cloth off, gave it a hem ripping snap and blubbered, "I'm always looking out for him." I sucked in some much needed air, flung some money in her direction, and fled.

Bertha belongs in congress and, like my dog, she has a license.

50

FROM TRAGEDY TO TRIUMPH

On Sunday evening, February 17, 1952 the service at Prays Mill Baptist church was in progress when the lights flickered off and on four times. Each blackout declared a death.

Pastor Carl J. Buice was preaching when our next door neighbor, Mr. Renzo Duren, exploded through the door and lunged down the aisle. One gallus on his overalls was fastened, the other bounced on his back. His house slippers slapped naked heels. His chin trembled and his voice cracked as he told us about the casualties. Four members of the Chapman family, our neighbors, had been electrocuted. Nine year old Ralph was the sole survivor.

A field at the corner of Big A road and Kilroy Lane had caught fire. The three Chapman boys, who lived nearby, raced to extinguish the grass fire. They assumed a careless smoker had caused it. But a 6,900 volt line had slipped from its anchors and sagged into the field. It grazed the ground and started the fire.

The circuit breaker failed. The wire was hot. Charles, the fifteen year-old, stumbled into the cable. Thirteen year-old Bryan tried to save his brother. Both were killed. Ralph attempted to pull Bryan off the wire. The power burned his hands but slammed him free. The father and mother, Tom and

Esther, heard Ralph's screams and rushed into the field. They were killed in a vain attempt to rescue their boys.

I went with my dad to the scene. The stifling smell of death hung over the field. Sheet shrouded bodies awaited J. Cowan Whitley, the undertaker. My eleven year-old mind clouded with gloom. Life had never seemed so uncertain nor eternity so sure as they did that somber Sunday evening.

On Wednesday, a throng, estimated at 2,000, assembled for the funeral at the Flint Hill Methodist church. Most couldn't get seats. Four caskets lined the front of the small auditorium. Reverends C.H. Smith, Selby Allsworth and Reuben Baxter read Scripture and tried to comfort friends and neighbors—and Ralph.

On Friday, *Douglas County Sentinel* writer, Marie Matthews wrote, "We trust time, love and sympathetic understanding will help him overcome the shock and grief experienced so early in childhood." They didn't.

Ralph endured a family squabble over custody that had to be settled in court.

The tornado of tragedy that swirled around the orphan embittered him toward God. He early sought solace in alcohol and drugs. By age thirteen he was an alcoholic.

Trouble trailed Ralph into manhood. Demonic twins, alcohol and drugs, swindled him out of hope and happiness. He and his wife lost three babies in a row. He was sinking in a sea of sorrow.

Then at age 30 a revolution reversed his life when he responded to a sermon entitled "There's Hope for the Hopeless". Jesus Christ swept into his life. A surge of peace cleansed, calmed and changed him. His testimony was that he never touched drugs, alcohol, or even said a swear word after that encounter.

For over 30 years he was a busy minister in Carroll County. He served as chaplain for the county jail, the county prison, the sheriff's department and the board of commissioners. He was responsible for 16 services each week.

Ralph identified with Psalm 40:2: *He brought me up also out of an horrible pit, out of the miry clay, and set my feet upon a rock, and established my goings.*

On Sunday, October 19, 2008 Ralph was promoted to heaven where he worships by sight the one whom he loved and served by faith for so many years

The victim of tragedies became the victor over trials. *". . . thanks be to God, which giveth us the victory through our Lord Jesus Christ."*

Edwards Brothers, Inc.
Thorofare, NJ USA
May 26, 2011